GROWING NEW CHRISTIANS

Books available in the CPAS series

A CPAS handbook

GROWING
NEW CHRISTIANS

Evangelism and Nurture in the local Church

Steve Croft

Marshall Pickering
An Imprint of HarperCollinsPublishers

Marshall Pickering is an Imprint of
HarperCollins*Religious*
Part of HarperCollins*Publishers*
77–85 Fulham Palace Road, London W6 8JB

First published in Great Britain
in 1993 by Marshall Pickering
1 3 5 7 9 10 8 6 4 2

Biblical extracts are taken from the New International
Version (NIV) copyright © 1978 by New York International
Bible Society, and are used in the United Kingdom
by permission of Hodder & Stoughton Ltd

A catalogue record for this book is
available from the British Library

ISBN 0 551 02701-6

Printed and bound in Great Britain by
HarperCollinsManufacturing Glasgow

Contents

PART FOUR **Resources**

Preface

"I tell you, open your eyes and look at the fields! They are ripe for harvest."

In every community in Britain today there are people who want to become Christians. The harvest is ready. This book has been written to give practical help to the harvesters.

Part One, Planning for Growth, offers a simple account of the way a person becomes a Christian and an outline of what is needed from the church at each stage of the journey. The model and strategy for evangelism and nurture in the local church is simple, tested in practice and effective in any situation with any type of church.

The main means of evangelism and nurture outlined is through groups. The remainder of the book concentrates on setting up and leading groups for evangelism and nurture in the church. Part Two, Planning for Groups, asks the preliminary questions. Part Three contains practical advice on leading the sessions. Part Four details resources and courses for group leaders and group members.

The aim has been to provide a practical handbook on helping people from unbelief to faith and through the first steps of their Christian life. The raw material for the book has been my own experience of leading Christians for Life groups within St George's Church, Ovenden, Halifax, over the last four years. About 200 people have taken part in these groups. Most are still growing in the Christian life.

Although the book is written within an evangelical Anglican perspective and in an urban setting, the principles given here do translate effectively into most other situations. It's my hope and prayer that *Growing New Christians* will prove useful to all flavours in the Church of England; to those within other denominations engaging in the same task; to those in rural and suburban settings; to small churches and to large ones; and to other groups, like Christian Unions, engaging in nurture.

I would like to express my thanks to Paul Simmonds of CPAS for his guidance, ideas and the writing stages; Tim Mayfield, Catherine Townend and other colleagues at St George's for encouragement, inspiration and support; my wife Ann, whose experience and ideas are as much a part of this book as my own; and to all those who have taken part in Christians for Life groups here over the last four years. To them and to the rest of the Christian family at St George's I dedicate this book with much love and with thanksgiving to God for their faith and love and prayer.

Steve Croft

PART ONE

Planning for Growth

1

Becoming a Christian

A process not a single event

Nicky is in her early twenties with a young son, Robert. She lives in the council estate in our parish and, until a few years ago, she had no Christian faith and no connection with the church. Over a period of several months, Nicky began seeking God. The Jehovah's Witnesses called and Nicky began to listen and to ask questions. She was walking in the park near our church one morning and "something" made her knock at the vicarage door and ask if she could come to church. She came the following Sunday, Easter Day, and was deeply moved, inwardly by the service and outwardly by the welcome she received. Nicky clearly wanted to know more straight away and a small team of people met with her over three or four weeks, began to get to know her, and explained the Christian Gospel in very simple terms. Nicky asked Christ into her life. The small group continued to meet with her for prayer and Bible study. Nicky joined the next Christians for Life group. She hadn't been baptized as a child so we borrowed our local Baptist church one evening for baptism by full immersion. Before Nicky was baptized she gave a very moving testimony of the change God had made in her life. She was confirmed shortly afterwards. Over the last few years there have been struggles, growth points, blessings, wounds in her life that have needed God's healing. Nicky is now established in faith and fellowship. She's part of our evangelism team, among other things; she's engaged to be married and still growing as a disciple of Jesus Christ.

Mark is an engineer, married to Debbie, in his early thirties and the father of two young children. Debbie became a Christian two years ago through contacts at school and in the church toddler group. Mark was hostile at first, then hesitant. He had everything he needed. Why did he need God? For a while he gave Debbie a hard time in her new faith. Then, from time to time, Mark began to appear in church. He came along to a couple of evenings arranged by Debbie's home group, he met the people and heard their stories. Almost reluctantly he agreed to join a Christians for Life group. All through the life of the group he asked question after question. As we talked and read the Bible together Mark realized that he was not quite the person he thought he was. At the end of the course, with just one other person present, Mark quietly made his own prayer of commitment. Like the rest of his story, nothing dramatic took place, but something very real had been happening over the months. At his confirmation, as Mark told his story, coming to faith had been like putting a jigsaw together one piece at a time, with God handing him the pieces. Since then Mark has gone on growing. He helps lead a group for men, he's co-led a Christians for Life group and is about to join a home group now.

Margaret is in her early seventies, though you'd never guess. Several years ago her husband died. Margaret had been a churchgoer earlier in her life and she began to attend a monthly family service in the small mission church near where she lives. When that church was closed a Christian neighbour brought her to St George's. A few months later Margaret joined Christians for Life. She asked more questions than anyone else I can remember. For Margaret there was no definite act of commitment made with anyone present, but she has testified many times: ''I thought I knew what it was to be a Christian; but I didn't know at all until I came to this group.'' Margaret was confirmed part way through the course. She loves children and she finds time now to help in the church playgroup and to teach the children on Sundays.

Eric is in his fifties and retired from work on health grounds. A year ago his wife died, suddenly and tragically of cancer. In the weeks following the funeral Eric began to come to church, initially to help his elderly mother-in-law who was already part of the congregation. Through the services and through members of the congregation, the Lord moved very beautifully in his life and Eric came back to the faith he had known as a young teenager. In the midst of his grief Eric found a deep joy and a peace which shines through him. His family wondered what had got into him but he kept coming. We had no Christians for Life group about to start and so Eric joined a new men's group and a home group. He was confirmed already and so he made a renewal of his baptismal vows at the next confirmation service. A few months later he joined Christians for Life, he became part of one of our teams working with the elderly and is now at the heart of the church family, growing in the faith.

For all of these people, and there are many others like them, becoming a Christian has not been a sudden, instant thing, a single event. Becoming a Christian is never a single, dramatic event (although many people's stories contain such events as part of a whole). Becoming a Christian is always a process. For most people that process begins long before there is any contact with a church.

Becoming a Christian is a process and understanding a little about how that process works is essential for any church or person engaging in evangelism or nurture. Despite the fact that the idea is clearly presented in Scripture and has been around in the modern church for some time, much outreach is still geared to an "event" conversion and an "after the event" pattern of nurture. The attitude prevails in tracts, in guides to evangelism, in missions of various kinds, in door-to-door visiting and in evangelistic services. Many missions, doorstep encounters and services are pitched towards that tiny minority of people who are actually ready to make a commitment to Christ at that particular time. Many nurture group strategies assume a group of newly committed Christians. Neither expectation is realistic. Becoming a Christian is a process.

The Bible uses a number of different pictures to describe this process of coming to faith. The most common are birth and child rearing, agriculture, gardening, building and the journey. None of these events is instant. Each has a number of stages. Birth is preceded by pregnancy and followed by infancy, childhood, adolescence and then maturity. There is no harvest unless there has been ploughing, sowing, weeding and growing (first the stalk, then the ear, then the full grain in the ear). There are no grapes without first establishing the vineyard and planting and tending the vine; no strong building without a foundation and so on.

However, by far the most common picture of the process of coming to and growing in faith is the picture of the journey. The whole Bible is a book of journeys, all of which have meaning: from Abraham leaving Ur; to the Exodus and Exile; to Jesus' journey to Jerusalem. The picture recurs in Christian writing in every generation and underlies much of the language of faith we use.

Understanding this book depends on understanding that becoming a Christian is a process, a journey. For the person on that journey to faith, different things will be helpful and appropriate at different stages on the journey. For the church which seeks to grow it is important to provide ways of moving on from every stage, not just from one or two points. Before that can happen we need some clear understanding of what the different points in the journey are and how we can describe them.

So how do we describe the different stages of the journey? No single model will cover every situation even for the stories of the four people told briefly above. One of the wonders of God is that he does not process us through some kind of spiritual sausage machine (although some Christians appear to think he does); he deals with us as individuals. Nevertheless, so long as exceptions are allowed, it can be useful to have models and stages of the journey to follow and to help us take others forward. I have found two such models to be especially useful. The first is based on the story of the two brothers in Luke 15. The second is loosely based on a scale developed by James Engel.

IMAGE	BIBLE REFERENCES	STAGES
BIRTH AND CHILD REARING	John 3:3–8 John 1:3 Titus 3:5 James 1:18 1 Peter 1:23 1 John 5:1 1 Peter 2:2 1 Corinthians 3:2 Hebrews 5:12–13 1 Corinthians 13:11 Galatians 4:19 1 Corinthians 4:15	Pregnancy Birth New born babies Infancy Childhood Maturity
AGRICULTURE	Jeremiah 4:3 Hosea 10:12 Mark 4:1–20 Mark 4:26–9 1 Corinthians 3:6,8	Ploughing Sowing Roots Shoots Weeding Stalk–ear–grain Watering Harvest
BUILDING	1 Corinthians 3:9–17 Ephesians 2:20–2 1 Peter 2:5 Matthew 7:24–7	Foundations Cornerstone Superstructure
GARDENING	Isaiah 5:1–7 John 15:1–8 Galatians 5:22	Planting Pruning Bearing fruit

The story of two sons

"There was a man who had two sons and the younger one said to his father . . ." Most readers will be familiar with the outline of the parable in Luke 15. The story is about the journey away from and back to God. With a little thought it is possible to discover eight different stages on the journey of faith within this one parable. I have found that people readily identify with one or other of these stages of the journey in a group context.

In most of our own groups we spend some time on the story of the two sons in about the second week, introducing people to the idea of journey and asking them to describe where they are in their walk with God. Time and again people have been set at their ease by this opportunity to describe the point they have reached in their own travels. I have frequently been surprised by the answers and always felt better enabled to lead the group forward because of what was so openly shared.

The eight stages in the story of the journey of faith are:

THE STORY OF TWO SONS

1. Running away

2. Living far away

3. Sensing your need

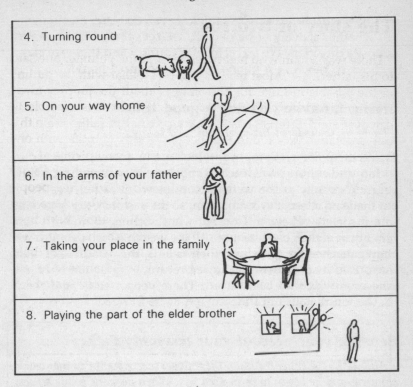

4. Turning round

5. On your way home

6. In the arms of your father

7. Taking your place in the family

8. Playing the part of the elder brother

Running away

"Not long after that, the younger son got together all he had and set off for a distant country . . ."

Many people begin their story by running away from the love of their heavenly Father. Perhaps in the teenage years, perhaps later, there is a flight from God; a rebellion against him. For some the rebellion is active. My wife was brought up a Roman Catholic and actively rebelled against the things her school and parents and friends had taught her in her early teens. It was six or seven years before she began her journey back to God again. For others the rebellion is passive. We just slip away. We can't be bothered to find out more. In all those years of rebellion we know, deep down inside, that God is there; we know the way we should go;

we know what he expects. We think we can do better on our own.
So, whether actively or by default, we set off or drift off in the
opposite direction. We travel to a far country and there we stay,
without so much as a phone call or a postcard home.

Living far away, having a good time

"There he squandered his wealth in wild living."

This is the point in the journey which many, many people in our
society and culture have reached and there they remain for many
years. As surely as the younger son knew his father was there
but made no attempt to contact him, so the vast majority of people
in our society believe in God but want nothing to do with him
other than at their convenience. All the wealth which people have
been given – all of their love, their talents, the resources of their
lives, the years which will never return – is squandered on
pleasures which are short-lived. There people settle and there
they often remain until they begin to be in need.

Sensing your need of your heavenly Father

*"After he had spent everything, there was a severe famine in that whole
country, and he began to be in need . . . When he came to his senses,
he said . . ."*

Time after time, what prompts people to move on in a spiritual
journey is an awareness of need in some form or another. Nicky's
story shows that well. At a certain point in her life she began to
be spiritually hungry. It was not until the younger son's natural
resources ran out that he began to think about his father. Even
then, because of his pride, he attempted to meet his own need
by every means possible, even lowering himself to feed the pigs,
before need drove him in the end to turn for home.

So often similar factors are operating today. People are shaken
out of their self-sufficiency by some spiritual or emotional need
and at those times begin to seek God. It may be a bereavement,
a problem in a relationship, a mid-life crisis, weakened health and

the sure knowledge that death is approaching, achieving life's goals and realizing there must be something more, depression of some kind, an awareness that you cannot bring up children by human standards. From time to time in all our lives we are brought face to face with our own frailty, our humanity and our need for God. It is at those times that we reach out and look for him and at those times especially that he is searching for us.

Turning round to come back

"I will set out and go to my father and say to him: Father I have sinned against heaven and against you. I am no longer worthy to be called your son; make me like one of your hired men."

A common point on the journey, after a person has realized their need for God, is the turning round to come back to him. Conversion means, literally, turning round, a change of direction. Conversion in this sense means the point at which you stop travelling away from God and begin the journey home. In a person's life it may be marked by very simple things: a desire to have a child baptized; or to begin attending church; a willingness to talk to Christians (if they know any) and to ask questions. The first steps are often very tentative. There is still some way to go before a point of commitment is reached, but the change of direction has already happened. It is at this point, very often, that a person will be ready to take part in an enquirers or nurture group.

On your way home

"So he got up and went to his father."

Those words contain a whole story in themselves. The son was in a distant country. The journey home would be neither short nor easy. Perhaps there were many distractions and stumbling blocks along the way; many times when the son's fear and shame at meeting his father outweighed his desire to be at home and he thought of turning back. In Bunyan's story of the journey,

Pilgrim's Progress, Christian has a whole series of encounters between his meeting with Evangelist and laying down his burden at the foot of the cross. For most people today, after the initial desire to turn round and seek God, will come the learning and discovering of the faith. The journey back is not, generally, the work of a moment. Help and guidance are needed each step of the way.

In the arms of your father

"But while he was still a long way off, his father saw him and was filled with compassion for him; he ran to his son, threw his arms around him and kissed him. The son said to him, 'Father . . .' "

The best part of the story is the picture of the gracious father still looking down the road after all of those years of his younger son being away. After the journey home, after the looking and the learning, comes the time for commitment and reconciliation of the person seeking God with the God who has been seeking him or her. It is one of the richest privileges of ministry to share in the joy of those times of reconciliation and commitment as person after person comes home to God. It is also very important, to change the metaphor to another Jesus uses, that people come to this new birth in a right and helpful way, and that we are effective spiritual midwives. There is more joy in heaven over one sinner who repents . . .

Taking your place in the family

The son comes home and there is reconciliation, feasting and a great celebration. If we take Jesus' story into the future, what would happen after the party is over? Things would not be as they were before when the son was at home. The younger son now needs to take his place again as a member of the family. He and his father will have much to talk about. He needs to work out his relationships to other members of the family. No doubt also, he needs to find his own place again in the work of the family on the farm. All of this will take time.

The parallels with our inner journey back to God are obvious. After a person has come home to the Father, there is and should be a period of rejoicing, not only for them but for the church or the small group. Then comes the period of taking his or her place as a member of the family once again; of deepening his relationship with God; of growing in relationship with older brothers and sisters; of beginning to find a place within the work of the family. As much help and care is needed at this stage of the journey as at any other.

Playing the part of the elder brother

There is one other place in the story we may find ourselves again and again in our Christian lives and that is in the place of the elder brother. He has lived at home so long that he now takes everything for granted. Everything that the father has is his. Yet his relationship with his father has declined and degenerated to one of work and service rather than love.

As Jesus tells the story, we are not told what happens to the elder brother. We leave him sulking outside the banquet, too proud to come in. Jesus means us to ask ourselves the question: will we enter into a fresh experience of the Father's love; or will we stay outside, sullen, jealous and angry; living among such riches but in reality so poor?

There are so many Christians, among them many who have worked hard in ministry, who find themselves in the elder brother's place in the story. Like the Ephesian Church we have laboured long and hard for the kingdom but we have lost our first love (Revelation 2:4). Part of the journey for those involved with nurturing new Christians will be discovering yourself in the elder brother's shoes and choosing once again to join the party. Part of caring for new Christians will be discovering that, surprisingly quickly, people can "graduate" to being elder brothers, unable to recognize that other people are now the focus of the attention, joy and celebration which they so recently enjoyed. Part of the challenge for any church which is experiencing significant growth and numbers of adults coming to faith is enabling the elder brothers and younger brothers to understand each other and to work together.

Stages on the journey

Although the story of the two sons is a very powerful story, it will not fit every situation. It can also be helpful in thinking through the process of evangelism and nurture to have a more systematic breakdown of the stages on the journey people often experience. This model is not quite so effective in sharing with people who are themselves at the beginning of the journey, but it is perhaps more useful to share with those who have the task of guiding them forward and planning the church's strategy and programmes for the task. The stages of faith here are loosely based on part of the Engel Scale, as adapted first by Eddie Gibbs and simplified and adapted again by me.[1] There are again eight stages, although they do not correspond at every point to the stages in the journey of the younger son.

Practical unbelief

Many people in our society have a mix of beliefs, of sorts, but are largely ignorant of what Christianity teaches and in practice see no need to do anything whatsoever about their faith. Time and again people have echoed Margaret's words to me: "I thought I knew what a Christian was until . . ." Within the range of people covered by the term "practical unbelief" there may be definite atheists, those who are openly agnostic and many who would describe themselves as Christian but whose Christianity bears very little resemblance to the faith as expressed in Scripture and the creeds.

An initial awareness of Christianity

Movement from the position often begins when such a person encounters Christianity for the first time and becomes aware that

STAGES OF FAITH
1. Practical unbelief
2. Awareness of Christianity
3. Wanting to know more
4. Discovering the facts
5. Admitting a need
6. Making a response
7. Established in relationship with God
8. Established in fellowship and ministry

there is such a thing as a living, Christian faith for adults for today. This may happen in a number of different ways, but is most likely to take place either through meeting someone who is already a Christian and unafraid to talk about their faith, or through a visit to a church. It may happen also through some outreach or mission event planned by the church. Up until that point a person may never have known that to have a living, growing, Christian faith and a relationship with God was even an option to consider for their own lives.

Wanting to know more

It is, of course, possible to know that the Christian faith is an option but to not want anything further to do with Christians, the church, or the Gospel. In our church, as most others, parents bringing children to baptism are asked to attend church for several weeks before the baptism service. All of these parents are given the opportunity to realize, through sharing in worship and encounters with the congregation, that the Christian faith is a living, vital option for today. Although some then do want to know more many, sadly, still slip quietly back into old routines once the baptism has happened. In the same way, there are many people who have close family or friends who are committed Christians. This group of people are aware that the Christian faith is an option for them but, for the present, simply do not want to know more.

That will always be the case for some. It is unrealistic to expect that everyone we are in contact with will want to go further. But we have found, increasingly, that the number of people who want to know more is growing all the time. The growth of the church is not limited by the number of people who want to become Christians. The growth is limited only by the rate at which we are able to teach, encourage and nurture new disciples and welcome them into the family. A lot of the work in the process of evangelism and nurture must be directed towards those who have had some contact with the faith and want to know more.

Discovering the Gospel

Commitment to Christ is about choice and decision; the greatest choice and decision we will ever make or ever ask others to make. Any choice or decision in life must be made on the basis of information. Therefore, between the stages of a person wanting to know more on the one hand and being invited to commit their life to Christ on the other, there needs to be a simple process of learning what the Christian Gospel is, in outline form.

The way and the rate at which this happens will vary enormously from person to person. For some, especially those with a good background knowledge of the faith from childhood, it really is sufficient for them to hear the Gospel explained once by a preacher or to read through an evangelistic booklet. In a way that no one can understand fully, the Lord brings all the threads of his search for them and theirs for him together in one encounter, and the process of discovering the Gospel and the claims of Jesus takes place in a moment. Like a man digging in a field, going about his everyday task, there is the sudden discovery of buried treasure.[2] The treasure is found by accident, recognized in a moment and the man acts immediately to lay hold of it.

I was walking home from the park one day when a man I didn't know pulled up in his car and asked directions to St George's Church. I introduced myself as the vicar and the man, who introduced himself as Ken, began to shed tears and asked if we could talk. We went back to my home and chatted as best we could while two of my children played. Ken was at a crisis in his life and was seeking God. I listened and said almost nothing. At the end of the conversation I gave Ken a copy of the small booklet, *Journey into Life*. Ken took the booklet away. We met later in the week and he told me he had read the booklet, said the prayer at the back with all his heart and from that point in his life began to change. Ken has now joined a Christians for Life group and is preparing to be confirmed.

That sort of encounter does happen once in a while. For others the discovery of the Gospel will be a more painstaking enquiry:

a step by step, stage by stage affair. Facts need to be uncovered. Questions need to be answered. Opinions and lives need to be tested out by long acquaintance. Long-held beliefs need to be discarded in favour of new ones. Past hurts on the part of the church may need to be forgiven. The cost of commitment needs to be weighed up. Like a merchant searching for fine pearls, for many the discovery of Jesus, the pearl of great price, comes after many hours of painstaking enquiry, questioning, reading and reflection.[3]

Charles has been coming to church ever since his wife came back to faith about a year and a half ago. He has had no previous contact with the church or the Christian faith at all. All the way through his search Charles has been willing to read, to take part in groups and to discuss. So far he's taken part in our men's group, watched most of the video series *Jesus, Then and Now*, listened to a variety of sermons and completed a Christians for Life group. As well as all that, there have been several one-to-one discussions until late at night with myself and Tim, my colleague. Only after all of that searching and questioning was Charles willing to place his faith in Christ and to say he is a Christian.

Others will be at every point in between Charles and Ken, but for everyone who makes the journey of faith at some point the learning needs to happen before a choice can be made.

Admitting a need

Alongside this process of outward discovery of the Gospel message there also needs to be an inward process of discovery of a person's own need for Christ. Without this, the outward learning will be irrelevant. No one is ever coerced into the kingdom. No one has ever been argued into the Christian faith by sheer weight of evidence either. There must always be a discovery of our own need for God and for Christ: that which an earlier generation of preachers called conviction. On several occasions I have known a man or woman join one of our groups for new Christians, sometimes under undue pressure from a relative or friend or even from myself. A process of learning has begun to take place, certainly. But there has been no corresponding recognition of need. Such people almost always fall away, either during the group or shortly afterwards.

This part of the process, even more than the other elements, is the work and preserve of the Holy Spirit. We are able to assist the process by our prayers, by teaching honestly about our need for God, by testimony and above all through exposing people to Scripture.

A response of faith

After the learning and awareness of need comes a response of faith. Again, however it happens, this seems to be an essential element in the process. At some point there needs to be an end to the period of seeking and enquiry, and a beginning to the process of growing in the faith. For some people, an act of commitment may be made in a very simple and private way, almost unrecognized. The author C. S. Lewis describes how, after months of searching for God, he got into a car saying he was not a Christian and got out of it at the other end saying he was, without really being able to analyse what had happened in between.[4] For others a commitment may be made in the context of a public service, either in response to an evangelistic appeal or through a baptism, confirmation or church membership liturgy. For many the context will be praying with one or two other people who are already Christians.

Becoming established in relationship with God

New Christians need particular guiding through the first few months of their Christian lives. In Luke 11:1 the disciples ask Jesus: ''Lord, teach us to pray.'' The request assumes that we learn how to pray – we are not born (or born again) with that natural capacity. There are things we need to know about worship; about its meaning and significance; about how to worship. There are good disciplines to be developed. People will need a great deal of help in understanding and appreciating the Bible. All of this needs time, pastoral care and a learning process for those who are new to the faith. To return to the picture of new birth, the need for spiritual midwives gives way to the need for spiritual health visitors and nursery teachers as the journey continues.

Becoming established in relationship with other Christians and in ministry

At this point a person's journey with God has only just begun. For most there will be many fruitful years of service ahead in service to the Lord they are growing to love. That journey will be lived out in the context of a local congregation. People need to learn certain things, therefore, in order to feel secure and take their place within the congregation. These include how to behave in certain situations, the story of the congregation, how to grow and move on in responsibility, and what their own responsibilities in the family will be with regard to prayer or giving or support for different activities. The congregation also needs to receive and welcome people, not just as newcomers (which most churches are good at) but as permanent members of the family (which is harder). The time that I most often see people standing on Sunday mornings with no one to talk to is not on their first or second visit, but after two or three months, when they are not "new faces" any more, but no one has really got to know them either. Becoming established in relationship with other Christians is as important as (and sometimes much harder than) becoming established in relationship with God.

Becoming a Christian then, is a process not a single event. The process can be described in different stages. Although no model will fit any or every situation exactly it is important when thinking through our evangelism and nurture structures that we have some idea what is taking place.

The next chapter will look at how the different activities within the life of the church can mesh with the process described here to build a strategy for growth.

Notes to chapter 1

1. Eddie Gibbs *I Believe in Church Growth* (London: Hodder & Stoughton, 1981), p. 223.
2. Matthew 13:44
3. Matthew 13:34–6
4. C. S. Lewis *Surprised by Joy* (London: Fontana, 1955), p. 189.

2

Involving the church at every stage

"I planted and Apollos watered, but it is God who gives the growth."
1 Corinthians 3:6

The importance of prayer

Evangelism and nurture is the task of the whole church, not simply the task of the clergy or of a small group within the congregation. In order to reach people at each stage of their journey it is necessary for the whole congregation to be committed to the process of growing, to the change that is necessary for growth to take place, and to the vital task of prayer for the growth to happen at all.

To return to the pictures of the harvest and the vine: there will be no lasting fruit unless and until the life of Jesus flows through the vine. It is God who gives the growth. In natural, human farming the growth happens automatically as the ploughing, sowing and weeding go on season by season. Many have testified, throughout the whole tradition of the Church, that this is not so in the spiritual harvest. For there to be spiritual growth, there must be prayer in the church; the branch must be abiding in the vine. If there is prayer, there will be life and growth of some kind no matter what structures and strategies are employed. If there is no prayer, there will be no life in the vine; there will be no growth no matter how many books are read or courses attended or structures changed. Without prayer, structures and strategies can be a dangerous distraction: changing them becomes simply a substitute for real achievement and fruit. The place for all of us and all our churches to begin the work of evangelism and nurture is the place of prayer.

The Scriptures and the whole spiritual tradition of the Church unite to teach us that this prayer must involve brokenness and repentance before God; ploughing up the fallow ground, to use the picture in Hosea and Jeremiah.[1] It is a sure spiritual principle, tested in many revivals, that this needs to happen before God will graciously bring a renewal of faith and life, first in the church and then in the community. Our own experience of growth bears this out. It is as the church prays that the growth begins to happen. When the church prays there is great sense of working with God in the field of human lives; there is a sense of wonder that God is moving in people in ways that we have not caused and could not have manufactured. But when the prayer is lacking the experience is that promised to Adam: much labour with only a little fruit.

The prayer that is offered needs to be deep, personal and persistent. The prayer needs to grow and deepen, we have found, as the life of the church grows and deepens. Some time ago Maureen, a member of our congregation, received a picture from God which summed up this process for our congregation. The picture is of two trees. The first is small, black and withered with roots penetrating just a few feet below the ground. The second is tall and luxuriant, full of fruit and colour and life. The roots of the second tree go as far down below the ground as the branches reach above it.

Through these pictures we believe that the Lord gave us a choice for our church. Which tree would we be like? The difference was not in our activities (the branches) but in the roots (the prayer). As the church grows larger, the prayer needs to go deeper. That demands time and faith and perseverance not just by a few, but by the whole church.

The place many churches will need to begin renewing and revising the process of evangelism and nurture will be prayer. For myself, I need to return here again and again and so does our church. If people are not willing to pray, that situation needs to be addressed first and foremost. If it is not, the result of new structures and groups will be frustration not fruit. Jesus promises to answer the prayers of his people. It is as we seek that we will find. We will not enable others to learn the way unless we ourselves are willing to pray.

For those who find a willingness to pray now in the church, but need some ideas about how to pray, the table gives some ideas about mobilizing prayer in the church. It may be that some of these would work in your situation. Generally speaking people do not just need to be motivated to prayer: we need practical suggestions about when and where to pray, together with accurate information about what to pray for and good feedback on prayer that has been answered.

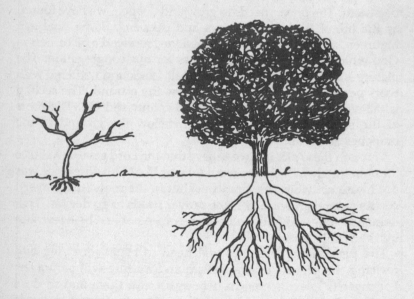

Figure 1: Prayer trees illustration

TEN IDEAS FOR BUILDING PRAYER IN THE CHURCH

1. A WEEK OF PRAYER January S 31 3 10 17 24 M 4 11 18 25 T 5 12 19 26 W 6 13 20 27 T 7 14 21 28 F 1 8 15 22 29 S 2 9 16 23 30	The church sets aside a week to pray at the beginning of the year. All normal activities are cancelled. There are meetings each evening led by different people. The aim is to centre the life of the church on the life of God at the start of a new year; to listen to the Lord for the way ahead and to intercede.
2. A DAY OF PRAYER **Saturday** **9** **MAY**	Effective for special projects (such as gift days), for special events (such as a mission) or special times of year (as at Pentecost). The day is twelve hours of prayer in church (8.00 a.m. to 8.00 p.m.). Each hour is led by a different home group or church leader. Each hour includes worship, Bible reading, listening and intercession.
3. A HALF NIGHT OF PRAYER	As for the day of prayer, only times from 6.00 p.m. to midnight, again divided into one hour slots.
4. A CHURCH PRAYER DIARY	Published monthly and issued only to those who sign up to receive the prayer diary and to pray through it. Ours is divided into three sections: part one gives specific prayer projects for that month; part two gives something in the life of the church to pray for each day; part three contains answers to prayer from the previous month. The diary is useful not only for individuals but for small groups meeting to pray.

5. TELEPHONE PRAYER CHAINS	Excellent for mobilizing prayer at short notice. Requests for intercessions (usually for the sick) are passed to a central person who clears the request with the vicar and activates the chains. Requests should be short and specific. Chains should be no longer than ten people (if you have more people it's best to have two or more parallel chains). Prayer should take place immediately the request is received if at all possible. Where possible again feedback and updated information should be given.
6. A PRAYER ROOM	A room on church premises set aside for prayer. People are encouraged to come and pray in the Prayer Room on their own or in small groups at a regular time each week. Requests for prayer can be updated through the prayer diary, blackboard or pinboard in the room.
7. PRAYER SUPPORT SCHEME P.S.S. I promise to pray for	Engaging in any ministry, especially in evangelism or Christian nurture, can be like entering a battle zone. Offering prayer support for those involved and their families is vital. In this scheme each person active in leadership or ministry is given three prayer support cards. These are given to friends in the church who undertake to pray for the person and their family regularly and for their ministry (see Colossians 4:12 for Epaphras' model of this).
8. SPECIAL PRAYER MEETINGS	Many churches have groups meeting to pray for specific areas of the church's ministry: for the healing ministry; for evangelism; for the Church overseas. Good information is essential. A number of teams in our own church responsible for particular ministries, such as work with the elderly or youth work, meet regularly to pray so that their own part of the church's life has this foundation. Other churches find monthly or fortnightly central prayer meetings important in encouraging prayer.

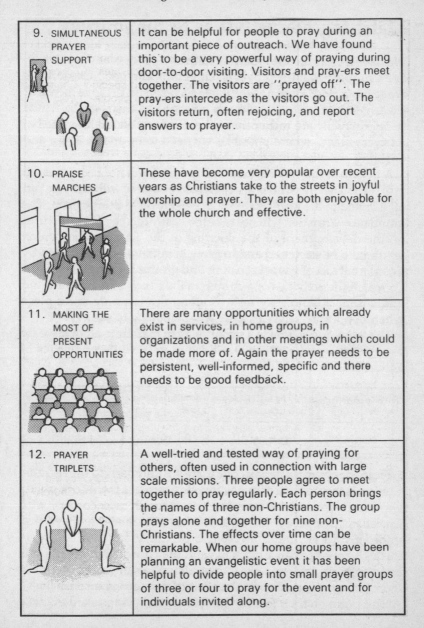

9. SIMULTANEOUS PRAYER SUPPORT	It can be helpful for people to pray during an important piece of outreach. We have found this to be a very powerful way of praying during door-to-door visiting. Visitors and pray-ers meet together. The visitors are "prayed off". The pray-ers intercede as the visitors go out. The visitors return, often rejoicing, and report answers to prayer.
10. PRAISE MARCHES	These have become very popular over recent years as Christians take to the streets in joyful worship and prayer. They are both enjoyable for the whole church and effective.
11. MAKING THE MOST OF PRESENT OPPORTUNITIES	There are many opportunities which already exist in services, in home groups, in organizations and in other meetings which could be made more of. Again the prayer needs to be persistent, well-informed, specific and there needs to be good feedback.
12. PRAYER TRIPLETS	A well-tried and tested way of praying for others, often used in connection with large scale missions. Three people agree to meet together to pray regularly. Each person brings the names of three non-Christians. The group prays alone and together for nine non-Christians. The effects over time can be remarkable. When our home groups have been planning an evangelistic event it has been helpful to divide people into small prayer groups of three or four to pray for the event and for individuals invited along.

Matching our activities to the journey

We have a clear picture, then, of faith as a process and a journey.
Let's suppose that the prayer is happening and people around us
are seeking God. How do we enable each person to move forward?
Clearly our activity as a church needs to be matched to where
people actually are rather than where we would like them to be.
At every stage, where possible, we need to be encouraging and
enabling people to move on in the right way.

A person at the stage of practical unbelief will not be impressed
by a tract. The one who is an interested enquirer will easily be put
off if linked to the well-established, weekly Bible study group. The
brand new Christian will not take too easily to a course of lectures
on the development of the doctrine of the Trinity. The person
wanting to be stretched and to grow in faith will be frustrated by
a continual diet of gospel sermons and groups for new Christians.
To match the activities of a church to the needs of people around
and within it is no easy task. Communication only takes place
when people are ready to hear what we have to say.

The following model is a simple way of matching all that we do
as a church in evangelism and nurture to the different stages of
a journey.

Practical Unbelief	Awareness of Ch'y	Wanting to know more	Discovering the facts	Admitting a need	Making a response	Relationship with God	Fellowship & ministry
CONTACT		EVANGELISM		NURTURE		GROWTH	

From the church's perspective there are four parts to the process.
Contact is the first. All of our evangelism remains ineffective unless
we are in touch with people. It is through real contact with
Christians that people are awakened or disturbed out of practical
unbelief into an initial awareness of Christianity. It is largely
through contact with Christians and the church that people will
move from an awareness of Christianity to an interest in learning
more (or not, depending on the effect of that contact on their lives).
At this point on their journey people are not being asked to make

a commitment to Christ, simply to "Come and see" (John 1:39); to look further and deeper at what Jesus says.

If this simple distinction between contact and evangelism is grasped, all of the "pressure" is taken out of evangelism, for the church and for those outside. Pressure, stress and guilt rebound on the church whenever part of what should be the contact process (an open-air service or some door-to-door visiting) is forced to bear the weight of the whole structure. This is perhaps the single biggest reason why the Church has been put off evangelism. Ways in which the local church can make contact effectively with the local community are outlined in chapter three.

Evangelism, the second part of the process, is not forcefully stating gospel summaries to those who do not want to listen. Evangelism is explaining the Christian faith and the Christian Gospel to those who want to know more. At this point on their journey people do need to discover something about sin; about Jesus' ministry, death and resurrection; about the gift of the Holy Spirit; and about their own need of God. That learning can take place in a whole variety of ways: through sermons; through one-to-one or one-to-two discussions; or through reading. In many churches that learning takes place best through a group – often the same group which is addressing the next part of the process.

Nurture follows evangelism. At some point a decision of commitment to Christ is made (for further discussion of this see chapter ten). Before, around and after this commitment there is a need for nurture: for teaching; for befriending; for incorporation into the body of the church both publicly and socially. There is a need for people to learn how to pray, about Holy Communion, about the Bible, Christian lifestyle and much more.

Again this nurture process can be helpfully carried forward in a number of ways from one-to-one teaching through to a formal class with many attending. Again, however, in most churches the small group is by far the best medium.

There is no straightforward, easily-defined division between evangelism and nurture. In most church situations therefore it is better for all concerned if one group fulfils both functions. It is the setting up and leading of these groups for evangelism and nurture combined which is the subject of parts two and three below.

The fourth part of the process on this simple model, the part which has no end, is growth. Every local church needs to provide the way and the means for people to grow in the faith and in their ministry. Most people in our situation go on from Christians for Life (our evangelism nurture group) to join one of the evening or daytime home groups. Some take part in other training and learning programmes within or outside the church. All leave the Christians for Life groups aware of the need to go on growing throughout their lives.

All of this translates into a very simple strategy for the church's mission of making disciples, and for church growth. At one end of the process are a variety of contact programmes. In the centre is one simple group, run as often as it is needed, for evangelism

Practical Unbelief	Awareness of Ch'y	Wanting to know more	Discovering the facts	Admitting a need	Making a response	Relationship with God	Fellowship & ministry
CONTACT		EVANGELISM		NURTURE		GROWTH	

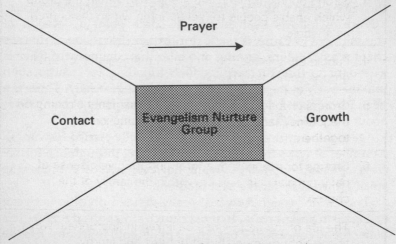

Figure 2: cracker structure

and nurture. At the other end are a whole variety of programmes within and outside the local church for going on growing. It is not hard to see that this cracker shaped strategy is there in embryo in many churches already. It is easily implemented, easily understood by most of the congregation and effective – through prayer and God's grace – because people are receiving the help they need at each point on their journey.

SEVEN REASONS FOR UNDERTAKING EVANGELISM NURTURE IN SMALL GROUPS
1. Small groups are more efficient in time and resources than one-to-one evangelism or nurture.
2. Groups are more effective as a teaching medium and give more scope for discussion, exercises, question and answer sessions, and feedback than one-to-one sessions or very large classes.
3. Strong bonds of friendship are formed within the group which enable people to feel at home within the church as a whole.
4. People are prepared for on-going membership of small groups within the church.
5. Groups give a general sense to the members of being on the journey (and at a similar stage in the journey) together.
6. Groups for evangelism and/or nurture give a sense of having a place as learners within the family of the church.
7. The life of the groups can be linked in appropriate ways to the right membership structures and liturgy.

42 *Growing New Christians*

SEVEN REASONS FOR UNDERTAKING EVANGELISM AND NURTURE IN THE SAME GROUP

1. People grow at their own rate within a group. Not everyone will have become a Christian by week six of an enquirers group (for example).

2. People who have become Christians before joining a nurture group (perhaps through an evangelistic service or booklet) still need a fuller understanding of the Gospel.

3. For a person on their way into faith and into the church, jumping between groups is hard. It is much easier and safer to be part of one group for the whole journey.

4. Group members will form deeper relationships the longer the group meets. If an enquirers group meets for six weeks (say), people will only be beginning to trust each other. The more people trust each other, the more will be shared. The more is shared, the more is learned.

5. One group for both purposes is much more efficient from the church's point of view, in terms of recruiting and training group leaders.

6. Some questions and themes can come up at any point in the course and be asked from an enquirer's or a non-Christian perspective.

7. In a mixed group of enquirers and new Christians, the best witnesses to the enquirers will be those who have recently come to faith themselves.

The model in practice

Ken had had no more than a passing interest in religion and in God for most of his adult life. Five years ago his eldest daughter came to be married in our church. To Ken's surprise, Janet and her fiance, Nick (whose great passion in life was his motorbike) began attending church regularly before and after the wedding. Nick and Janet joined the first ever Christians for Life group at St George's shortly after their wedding. Ken was sceptical, even after they had been confirmed, but he began to come to church himself, first occasionally and then more regularly. Again to his surprise, he found the natives friendly and the worship to his liking.

In due course both Ken and Joan, his wife, received an invitation to Christians for Life. Joan accepted. Ken declined – he wasn't going to go any deeper just yet. Each week, as the course unfolded, Joan came home buzzing with what had been said, what had happened, and the hand-out for that week. Ken discovered he looked forward to his Thursday late-night discussions with Joan as much as Joan herself was looking forward to the group. Halfway through the course, without being asked again, Ken offered to be part of the next Christians for Life group.

The first night came round. Everyone was nervous, even the vicar who was leading the group. There were about fifteen people in the group, meeting in the dining room of the vicarage. There were small group discussions, some input which made you think, a chance to ask any questions you liked and a good discussion. After the strangeness of the first meeting, Ken enjoyed the group enormously. He learned and understood the Gospel. His own need of God was growing. At some point in the course Ken made his own quiet and personal commitment to Christ. God was acting in his life in all kinds of ways. Ken already had a good discipline of Sunday worship. His appetite for meeting with other Christians deepened through the group. Ken began to pray and read the Bible, finding things hard at first. It was some comfort to know that others in the group had the same problem as he did.

From the Christians for Life group Ken easily made the transfer to a home group. Joan had already joined and made friends there. Several years later Ken has grown and matured in faith and would say he is still growing and learning; active in ministry and drawing others to Christ.

Kath works behind the check-outs in Sainsbury's. She's married with two children and was in the same Christians for Life group as Ken's wife, Joan. Kath has a Roman Catholic background but had lapsed from her own faith when she was young. Kath began attending St George's most weeks in 1987. It wasn't until two years later that she felt ready (or wanted) to join a Christians for Life group. Coming to church was enough. At the group itself she was very hesitant, wary of getting "too much religion". Through the teaching and discussions, through the questions and the friendships she formed, Kath's whole understanding of Jesus and the Christian life broadened and deepened. She began to hear God's call on her life in a much deeper way. For the first time Kath heard and understood about the life of the Holy Spirit. She opened her heart and life to Christ and he came in, filling her with the Spirit. As so often, it was like a light had been switched on inside. The group gave her good teaching on living the Christian life and on prayer. The growing went on as Kath became a member, then a co-leader, of a home group. Stephen, her husband, became a Christian in his own way earlier this year and is a member of a Christians for Life group himself now. From very slow and hesitant beginnings Kath's faith has grown and matured and is bearing much fruit.

Linda, who also works in Sainsbury's, was part of St George's as a teenager. She wandered away, lived with her boyfriend for a while, became pregnant, split up with her boyfriend and went back to live with Mum. When Bradley was born, Linda just knew, somehow, that it was time to come back to church. She brought Bradley for baptism. As part of the baptism preparation, Linda met several members of the church and began to see that there was more to the Christian faith than she'd realized until now. She was invited to a Christians for Life group, during the course she made a commitment to Christ and was confirmed. Since then there have been ups and downs; struggles and joys. Linda is still part of a home group, co-leads Christians for Life groups, and is part of our baptism team herself now.

Everyone's story is different and individual. Each journey has its own twists and turns which make that road unique. Yet it is possible within all of these different journeys to distinguish different stages. People pass through those stages at different rates and sometimes in a different order. The church needs a simple, flexible structure which can adapt to different people's needs and enable each one to move on.

The cracker shaped model described here works in all kinds of situations. There is always a need for contact, evangelism, nurture and on-going growth. Through the structures we offer, through the planting and the watering, God goes on giving the growth.

Note to chapter 2

1. Jeremiah 4:3; Hosea 10:12

3
Making contact with those outside

Any church which desires to grow needs to be in contact with a growing number of people who are not Christians. It sounds so obvious as to be hardly worth stating yet the point is often missed by leaders and by congregations.

Imagine a small church of about forty adult members which is engaging with the decade of evangelism. Visitors and new people hardly ever appear in the congregation. Energy is limited, so almost everything which happens within the life of the church is geared to those on the inside. The people mix mainly with each other: few meaningful relationships are formed with those who are not Christians. This means in turn that the language of this little community becomes more and more religious, specialized and in a code those outside cannot understand. The result is paralysis. The church cannot grow because there are no meaningful contacts with non-Christians. At the same time the small group is becoming harder and harder to break into from the outside. Losing contact with the community is the first step on the road to the death of a church; regaining effective contact with the community can be the first step to recovery.

How is that contact made and maintained? There are different ways. Some will be right in one situation, others in another. What is important is that this process of contact is happening somehow. This chapter looks at five different ways of making contact and concludes with a look at four different stepping stones: ways of sharing the Gospel with people before they are ready to come to an evangelism nurture group.

Through Sunday worship

For many the most important area of contact is through visitors to church on Sundays. This is the case in our own situation. There is hardly ever a Sunday when there are not visitors, newcomers or strangers within each of the church services. For most congregations worship will be the shop window for the faith. A surprising number of people do come window-shopping. It is enormously important therefore that our church services are accessible to newcomers; that they are well-publicized; that we are user-friendly in our approach to worship; and that what is offered Sunday by Sunday is not only of the highest possible standard, as it is offered to God, but that it is attractive to those who are outside the church.

This means many different things in practice: paying attention to detail is important. Remember to announce page numbers so people can follow the service. Heat the building properly. Try and see things through the eyes of the visitors. Explain things that may seem strange or unfamiliar within the worship. Over and over again, however, people who have become Christians through visiting our own church (and other churches I have known) have commented on three things which have attracted them and have made them want to return.

The first has been the welcome by the existing congregation. It is very difficult, if not impossible, to come in and out of our church on a Sunday without being greeted and spoken to by several people. That doesn't mean that the visitor is smothered. The welcome is rarely intrusive into a person's privacy. It does mean that genuine love and care is shown to the guest and the stranger. People's stories indicate that, sadly, this is a rare experience for them as they have visited other churches and congregations. The expectation of the wider community is that if you come to church, no one will even speak to you. What an indictment of the church of Jesus Christ! Some churches have found highly-trained welcome teams to be effective. In our own situation we have stewards on the doors, but the main welcome is left to the congregation as a whole. Everyone is involved. Coffee after the services is a part of the whole process of welcoming. It's there, very often, that conversations begin and people realize that the love which is offered is not limited to a cheery greeting once a week but to a real concern for their lives.

The second ingredient in our own worship which people have found attractive is the style of the worship itself, especially the music. Like many churches, we have a mix of music now: some older hymns with organ accompaniment but mainly modern worship songs led by a music group. The music is in contemporary style and continually surprises and delights the visitors who come to worship. The words of many of the modern songs express an intimacy and depth of love for God which many find moving. The music, sometimes lively and sometimes gentle, is the sort of music people are used to hearing all week long outside of church. The songs are easy to learn and easy to sing. It's worth saying that often it is the older visitors who are particularly surprised and delighted. Over and over again I have heard people say that the reason they do not come to church is not because they don't believe but because the services are so boring. The style of music in a church is often one of the hardest things to change. It is also one of the most important if the congregation is going to reach out and if the services are to be an effective way of making contact.

The third element which people mention which attracts them is the preaching. People are surprised that the sermon can be easy to listen to, relevant to their situation in life, enjoyable and challenging. Time and again people have said: "It's as though the preacher was speaking directly to me. How did you know?" Developing a welcome in the congregation, changing the music and developing preaching skills are all outside the scope of this book, but they are mentioned because each is relevant to the process of making contact with the wider community through our weekly worship.

Special services also provide opportunities for contact with many more people than the Sunday congregation: at festivals such as Christmas, Harvest, Mothering Sunday and Easter, and on other special occasions. Imaginatively used, they can be ways of demonstrating to the wider community that Christianity is alive; that through Jesus God changes lives, and it is worth looking further to find out more. The whole gospel does not need to be presented to the newcomer on every occasion. What is important is that people are moved on from practical unbelief to an awareness of Christianity and, hopefully, from there to wanting to know more. Special guest services too can be effective.

One lesson we have learned in all of this is that, while it is important that our services are accessible to newcomers, it is a mistake to gear them simply to the needs of newcomers. Services of worship are an encounter between the living God and his people. In the end it is the integrity of the worship and of that encounter which will attract, not any amount of gimmicks.

Through the occasional offices

Any church, especially an Anglican parish church, comes into contact with many families through baptisms, weddings and funerals. There are opportunities which come through each of these offices for teaching, for preparation, for on-going contact and pastoral care which we are rarely able to make the most of. Again it is important to remember that many people will judge the church by these occasions. The clergy bear a particular responsibility here. Too often people are met with a rudeness and abruptness on the telephone or doorstep which would be severely reprimanded in many major companies. The condition of the church building speaks volumes about the life of a congregation. The attitude of the church to outsiders coming in to use the building will be perceived by the community. Are our doors open, or are they seen to be closed?

The kind of baptism policy a parish adopts is vitally important. Although a closed baptism policy may be theologically satisfying to clergy and people it will be pastorally disastrous. Nothing alienates communities and parishes more effectively than a stark refusal to baptize the children of that community which, however disguised, is almost always perceived as rejection. It is important when people make their first tentative approach to the church that we are heard to say "Yes", rather than "No". In our own situation when a person asks for baptism the reply is always "Yes", then we explain that the parents will need to come to church for six weeks before we can set the date, and that there will be preparation evenings. People can see, in this context, that our request is reasonable. If they are not able to make that effort to come to church for a short time, then that is their decision.

If the ministry to those who contact us for occasional offices is seen as part of a process, a great deal of pressure can be removed in those situations. We are no longer seeking new Christians directly from baptism preparation meetings, or pre-marriage interviews, or from contact with the bereaved. Experience teaches us that this is very rare in any case. We are seeking, once again, to make people aware of what the Christian

---

BAPTISM ENQUIRIES: AN OUTLINE PROCEDURE

1. Initial contact by the family to the vicar.

2. Clergy visit. Alternatives of baptism and thanksgiving explained. Family invited to church.

3. Visits to church over six weeks.

4. Home visit by baptism preparation team.

5. Preparation meeting for parents and godparents led by the team.

6. The baptism (in context of morning service).

7. Follow up visit by the baptism team. Invitation to go deeper if that seems right.

8. Long-term follow up by the church pastoral team, keeping in contact once or twice a year.

faith is, and we are seeking to identify those who, at this stage in their lives, would like to find out more. It is important that we then have the means to enable them to travel further.

Through community programmes

Community programmes are important in the life of the church for their own sake. We have Jesus' commission to love our neighbour as ourselves which applies to churches as much as to individuals. Caring for the community also lends a basic integrity to our evangelism. If all that the church offers is an endless stream of invitations to special services we are not reflecting the Gospel. The message caught by the community will be that the faith is simply about coming to church and being part of a religious club. Faith must be expressed in action.

Community programmes are also a very important means of contact between the faith community and place community. The list of potential community programmes is vast: groups for mums and toddlers, playgroups, luncheon clubs for the elderly, self-help groups for the disabled, drop-ins for the unemployed, uniformed groups for children, open youth work. All of these ventures are excellent in themselves. Different activities will be right for different churches in different situations. All of them serve to bring Christians and the church as a whole into meaningful contact with those who are, as yet, outside.

If the groups and programmes are to serve this purpose effectively, it seems to me to be very important that ventures mounted by the church should be seen as Christian outreach, and should therefore be staffed and led by those who are already Christians. All too often churches mount community programmes, which are excellent in themselves, but then surrender the evangelistic potential by involving those who are not members of the church at the heart of the work. The central task of the church is to make disciples. It is better, in my own view, to have a small number of activities (or perhaps only one activity) which is staffed by Christians than a whole range of events where the Christian commitment of the leaders is vague or non-existent.

Somewhere in the aims of each group, whatever the activity, should be the desire to make disciples. The programmes and activities need to be supported and earthed in prayer by the team involved. The teams need to be aware of the overall vision of the church and to know how their own activities fit in with other events within its life, especially with the strategy for evangelism and nurture outlined above. If possible, the teams also need some training in sharing their own faith simply within these situations, and in seeking to recognize people who are becoming aware of what Christianity is and want to know more.

Faith sharing in these situations can be done in a number of ways. A number of people have become Christians in our own church over the last few years through contact with our mother and toddler groups. One of the initial aims of the groups was to provide the best possible parent and toddler facilities for the people of the area. Each group is staffed by three or four Christian women. Faith sharing takes place within the group in a very natural and unforced way: through sharing of people's stories; through the lending of books; through occasional invitations to special events; through practical caring and listening. All such groups take time to establish. At one time we were in contact with about six mums. Now the groups bring the church (and Christians) into contact each week with over sixty families. A bridge is being built and relationships established which can be a channel for the Gospel.

Through personal contacts

Let's assume there are sixty people in your church by now (assuming a little growth has taken place because of all the changes). Let's assume that each of these people knows at least twenty others who are presently outside the church (some will know more, but others less). These people may include family members, neighbours, colleagues, parents of children's friends and so on. This means that as a congregation you are already in meaningful contact with over a thousand people in your community without any specific advertising or organized event. Experience suggests that from within that group of a thousand people there will be many who are already at a point in their lives where they want to know more about the faith. The whole congregation need to be encouraged to be willing to share their own faith in a natural and authentic way, not through pressure selling, but as opportunity arises.

I have the feeling that when many congregations are encouraged to evangelize the net result is guilt and frustration – even withdrawal – rather than faith sharing. The reason for this is partly that evangelism is generally portrayed only as activity at stages four, five and six of the stages of faith – especially six. These stages, generally, require more understanding of the faith and skills in communication which people feel they lack. Success is perceived as leading a person in an act of commitment to Christ.

We need to develop a much more healthy view of evangelism which sees basic witnessing to the faith in everyday life as the rightful preserve of every church member. In practice this means people living out their Christian life wherever God has called them to be: loving those around them; being prepared to pray for their non-Christian friends; to tell their own story of faith naturally when opportunity arises; and being prepared to point people in the right direction when they want to know more. This may mean lending books, an invitation to services or to a group. Success must not be seen as praying prayers of commitment with people. If we need to have a concept of success at all (and I suspect most of us do, however suspicious we may be of the term) it should be that of moving people on in their search for God; helping them forward on the journey.

Helping the congregation to play their role as witnesses needs to be an increasing theme through the decade of evangelism. This can be done effectively through whatever channels for teaching and training exist within the life of the church: through sermons, special courses, home groups, etc. We have found especially helpful here parts of the Bible Society/Scripture Union publication *Person to Person*.

Through outreach events

The circle of contacts any church has already will be large. But there will be those in any community who, at present, are right outside any meaningful contact with the faith. Outreach events serve to make those contacts and give the invitation to be disciples to a wider group of people still. Events of this type include open-air services, holiday clubs, door-to-door visiting, pub work; again, the range is wide. We need to be realistic about our expectations. It is very rarely (though not unknown) that a person will make a commitment to Christ through an encounter with open-air street theatre or from a cold visit. When that does happen, they have normally been drawing closer to God in their own journey for some time already. But does this mean that such events are a waste of effort? Not at all. Once again people are enabled to move on in the journey. An encounter with lively Christian music, Christians who look "normal", and street theatre which makes you think in the main precinct of your town will make anyone who has written Christianity off sit up and take notice. A visit to your home from the local parish church – even if you don't want to talk about religious things – lets you know that the church is there; the people who go are not much different from you; and they are bothered enough to come to see you. Perhaps you will give it a try, one day soon . . .

Any evangelistic event with the limited aims of making people aware that the church is there and cares, and with the hope that some will be attracted and want to know more, is almost bound to succeed and meet those aims. Most evangelistic events with the unrealistic vision of many people coming from unbelief to faith in one brief encounter will be affected by that pressure for "results" and will end in frustration. The church won't want to try again for some time. Often the feeling after such an event is "What did we do wrong? Perhaps we didn't pray enough." Often the expectations of the event were simply too high. No one wants to put energy and time into something which doesn't work.

Earlier this year we began a series of Making Contact missions in our parish. We hope to run two each year during the decade

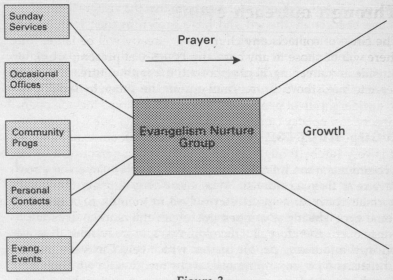

Figure 3

of evangelism. The idea is to take a small area of our community and to visit every home over a period of two weeks. A small team of visitors is drawn together and trained over three evenings before the event. The mission is preceded by a praise march through the area on a Sunday afternoon. Leaflets are delivered telling people what is happening. The visitors go out with the aim of simply making contact with people in the community and letting them know we are here. One or two events are held in the area or at the church to coincide with the mission. In the second event we had the aim of establishing a daytime enquirers group within that particular area of the parish.

The overwhelming response to the visitors has been positive. There have been some rude people and some who simply didn't want to know. But the majority were delighted and surprised to receive a visit from their local church. Each series of visits has thrown up fifty or sixty contacts to be followed up at a later date: baptism enquiries; enquiries about toddler groups or centres for the elderly; people wanting to know more about the faith; pastoral needs. The other direct result has been that the visitors themselves have been strengthened and have grown in their faith and in confidence in the Gospel.

We have now put flesh on the bones of the first part of the cracker structure. In diagram form the five main ways of making contact are shown in the drawing on the previous page.

Four stepping stones to faith

Sometimes when we make contact with people outside the church it's clear they do want to know more or go further. They may not be ready to commit themselves to coming to a group of strangers which is going to meet for several months. It has been important, therefore, to develop ways of communicating the Gospel and taking people further which come between making contact and joining an evangelism nurture group. Four ways have been important:

Through personal evangelism

Diane has a Roman Catholic background and first came into contact with St George's through meeting mums at the nursery unit. From there she began to attend one of the toddler groups and made several new friends who were Christians. Two of the friends, Ann and Debbie, were able to talk to Diane about their faith and tell their own stories. Diane became more interested and was keen to read some Christian books, which she borrowed. It was hard for Diane to come to church and to group meetings because of her work shifts and other factors. Eventually, without ever coming to a church service, Diane reached the point where she knew she wanted to become a Christian. Ann and Debbie met with her one evening and went through a simple gospel booklet, *Knowing God Personally*. Diane asked Christ into her life and began to grow as a Christian. After a while, disciplines of worship began to form and Diane, with Brian her husband, joined Christians for Life.

Personal evangelism can only take place in the church if there are people willing to share their faith and able to do so in a natural and attractive way. This will not be everybody's gift — but it will be somebody's! The natural, personal evangelists within any group or congregation need to be encouraged and equipped for the task. A course like *Person to Person* (in our case extensively adapted) can be ideal for this. But a word of caution is needed. Not everyone in a congregation, group or team is an evangelist. We have found by experience that a course like *Person to Person*, or any evangelism training used in home groups, has a negative as well as a positive effect. People begin to feel very guilty and second-class because they simply are not evangelists. It's much better to run a faith-sharing course independent of any existing group or structure, for those who want to go further.

Through guest services or meetings

These can be very effective, providing the congregation or organizing group are prepared to support them in prayer and by their presence, and are prepared to take the risk and bring people along.

Open House evenings have developed as part of the life of some of our home groups. Once or twice a year the group arrange a simple supper party for family and friends who are not Christians. Invitations are printed giving the time, date and venue. The ticket says clearly that, "The evening will include supper and a short presentation about the Christian faith." The event begins with the food. At a certain point the group leader or staff member calls things to order and co-ordinates a very simple presentation. This consists of two or three testimonies from members of the group, possibly followed by some discussion in twos and threes. The presentation lasts about twenty minutes and ends with an invitation to find out more by coming to Christians for Life, a guest service or some other event. The evenings bear fruit in terms of new people coming in and also have the effect of stretching the faith of the home group.

Larger, centrally organized events also have their place, either for the whole church or for a particular age group. A group within our church found a book by Rita Nightingale very effective in personal evangelism.[1] The group wrote to Rita and asked her to come and speak. Many who had read the book came along on the evening arranged and several became Christians. Others moved on in their journey. Each event, whether large or small, is like a stepping stone on the way from unbelief to faith.

Through evangelistic home visits

One of the best places of all to share the faith with people is within their own homes. A number of ways of doing this have developed over the last decade, based upon Michael Wooderson's scheme, *Good News Down the Street*.[2] Our own version of this, developed by my colleague Tim Mayfield, is called Open Door.

Invited people from the congregation are trained for six weeks in sharing the faith and using the material. The trainees then join the "pool" of the wider Open Door team.

People on the fringe of the church who seem to want to know more – but who don't seem quite ready for a Christians for Life group – will be asked if they would like to receive a team within their home for three evenings. The team consists of three people for a couple, and two people of the same sex for a person on their own. A different team is drawn together from the wider pool for each situation, depending on circumstances and the availability of team members.

The team then visit the person at home for three evenings over a three week period. Week one is a chance to meet and get to know each other. Members of the team share their testimony and listen to what the person is saying about his or her own journey of faith. In week two the team present a very simple outline of the Gospel and end with an invitation to think this through in the week ahead. In week three there is a chance for people to pray a prayer of commitment with the team and receive some very basic help in worship, prayer and Bible reading. Alternatively week three can be a chance to ask questions and talk further. Open Door is fairly open-ended, in that visits can continue for as long as the team and the people being visited find them worthwhile. For those who respond to the Gospel, the aim is to establish them in faith and link them in with the next Christians for Life group. For those who do not respond the aim is to help them to go on thinking and leave them an opportunity to come back in the future.

Through short-term enquirers groups

From time to time a group will emerge within the church or on the fringe which is simultaneously interested in going further. They may not be ready or willing to come to Christians for Life, but may well appreciate some kind of short-term enquirers group. One such group in our own parish has come out of a Making Contact mission on one of the council estates. Another, with the name "Real men don't go to church", was helpful to a group of men in the church who were new Christians or on the edge of faith. Others could fruitfully develop in the future among toddler and playgroup mums or with the elderly, as resources and people are available.

Christ Church, Bridlington, have developed a very flexible system of short-term enquirers groups, called Alpha groups. They can be set up and run by any member of the church and are overseen and supervised by the different house groups in the church. At present there are Alpha groups meeting in different areas – in a factory, in a college – wherever there are two or three people who want to learn.

The material used in these groups varies. Video can be used to good effect, as can written course sheets, but the overriding emphasis needs to be discussion related to where people are. In our own situation, and at Christ Church, people can be encouraged to move on to an evangelism nurture group or, in certain circumstances, the enquirers group can itself develop into that new kind of group as faith and trust grow.

Again we can put flesh on the bones of the simple cracker structure as the stepping stones come between contact programmes and the evangelism nurture group. These stepping

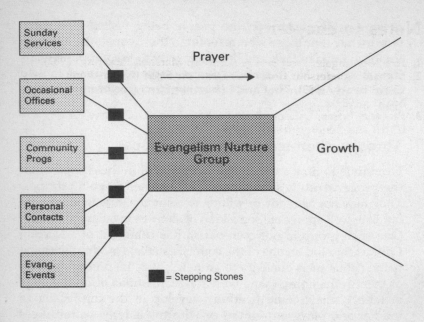

Figure 4

stones are not essential – not every church will have the resources
to provide any of them. Four years ago we had none in place in
our own situation yet people were still willing to come to
Christians for Life. Many people still join a Christians for Life
group here without passing through any of the stepping stones
outlined above. But while the stepping stones are not essential,
they are very helpful – particularly for those who show some
interest but need encouragement to go further.

Part one of *Growing New Christians* has covered planning for
growth. Part two goes on to focus on setting up groups for
evangelism and nurture within a church, and looks at the different
questions which need to be asked and answered for the groups
to be effective there.

Notes to chapter 3

1. Rita Nightingale, *Freed for Life* (London: Marshall Pickering, 1982).
2. Michael Wooderson, *Good News Down the Street* (Nottingham: Grove Books, 1983), *The Church Down our Street* (Eastbourne, MARC, 1989).
3. *Person to Person*, London, Bible Society, Campus Crusade for Christ and Scripture Union, 1986.

PART TWO

Planning for Groups

4
Church size and church growth

No two churches are the same. They vary in size, in social context and in questions of churchmanship and worship as well as other areas. Groups for evangelism and nurture are essential in any congregation which desires to grow. But no single prescription for a group can meet every situation. A group in a church of thirty members needs to be different from a group in a church of three hundred. A group held in the stockbroker belt in Surrey will need to be different from a group in a mixed-race area of Birmingham. A group held in an Anglo-Catholic parish, which has a strong theology of the church and where all the important aspects of common life are expressed in the liturgy, will be different from a group in a charismatic-evangelical church which sits loose to tradition.

These differences need to be recognized. Evangelism nurture groups need to be related carefully to these three variables: the size of the church; the wider social context; and the way the life of the group is linked to the liturgical life of the church. This chapter and the next look at each of these three areas and offer practical suggestions for different situations.

Different sized churches grow in different ways. There are several ways of dividing up churches according to size. To keep things simple, I suggest four sizes of congregation: small, medium, large and very large. These correspond to the four descriptions of church size in a booklet by Arlin Rothauge *Sizing up the Congregation for New Member Ministry*.[1] Rothauge's division is:

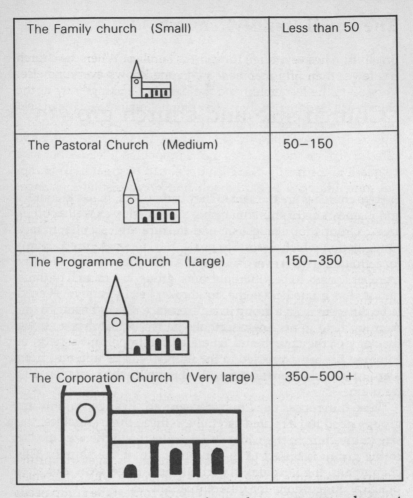

The Family church (Small)	Less than 50
The Pastoral Church (Medium)	50–150
The Programme Church (Large)	150–350
The Corporation Church (Very large)	350–500 +

For our purposes, numbers refer to the average attendance at Sunday worship. Rothauge's booklet has a detailed analysis of each size of church, how each type might attract new members, and how new people can be helped to feel at home. I have adapted the model here to a discussion of the place of evangelism nurture groups within each size of church and how the role of the groups changes as the church grows.

The small (family) church

Small churches very often function as families. When the church has fewer than fifty members, everyone knows everyone else. Very often the leadership and the decision-making body of the church will be dominated by a few human families who have held office for several generations. The minister or priest in such a situation may well be part-time or have other congregations to care for. He or she functions not so much as a leader but as a chaplain to the family. Small churches can be great to be part of but sometimes can be hard to join and very resistant to change. Whilst much of the energy of church members will be focused inwards, there will be some within the family who are natural welcomers: people who are good at helping the new member feel at home and introducing them gradually to the rest of the congregation.

Small churches need to recognize their God-given strengths and also their limitations. There is a great need to focus energy and to avoid the temptation to imitate and reproduce the life of larger churches in a way that simply will not work. A small church will not be able to take on many contact projects: it is better to specialize and do one or two things well rather than attempt a whole range of activities badly. There may not be the energy or time available to develop any of the stepping stones described in the last chapter (although one or two teams on the Open Door model would be useful). It may be possible to look to larger churches in the area for ideas and for training.

However, it ought to be possible to run an evangelism nurture group at least once a year, perhaps combining with other small churches in the area. In the small church context the group needs to contain several established members and leaders of the church so that new members can get to know the senior members of the family and vice versa. In some cases leadership of the group will be best in the hands of these senior lay leaders, with the minister in a visiting and monitoring role. In other situations the leadership will be best left to the minister with established church members there as helpers. Having new and established people together is vital. Not only do new members feel welcomed by the existing congregation but the established church family are not suddenly threatened by lively groups of new Christians who are known to their minister but not to them. Suspicion and mistrust cannot grow as easily in a place where both groups are learning together.

The on-going growth programmes will also need to be a mix of new and old, with one or two home groups and perhaps an occasional special course or conference. The evangelism nurture group needs to begin with the most basic input and questions – especially if people are joining without any stepping stones to faith. The group members need to be prepared carefully for membership of home groups, or (perhaps better) the group can be established as a new home group led by people who have been part of the group, as more mature Christians, from the beginning.

The other important benefit of keeping old and new church members together in the groups is that the faith of the long-standing church members will be enlivened and renewed by contact with people who are becoming Christians or those new

---

FEATURES OF AN EVANGELISM NURTURE GROUP IN A SMALL CHURCH

1. Run infrequently (once a year) because of resources and a smaller number of contacts

2. Possibly a joint group with other small churches

3. Should contain a mixture of established church members and new Christians/enquirers

4. Needs to begin with very basic questions (no stepping stones)

5. Led either by minister or established lay leaders

6. Best to continue as a new home group in its own right, if possible

to the faith. As mentioned already, the elder brothers will need special care here.

Small churches are able to grow with prayer and care. As in other contexts, a group for evangelism and nurture will be central.

St James the Less, a "traditional" Anglican church, has about thirty adults who regularly attend worship on Sundays. The church is in a small village close to a larger city. Many young families have been moving into the area recently. The new people have no way of meeting each other. The church is also receiving an increasing number of baptism enquiries. After prayer and thought the church decides to concentrate outreach among these young families. A small number of younger, married couples who are already Christians have moved into the area and are willing to help with this.

Sunday worship begins to change with an all-age worship service

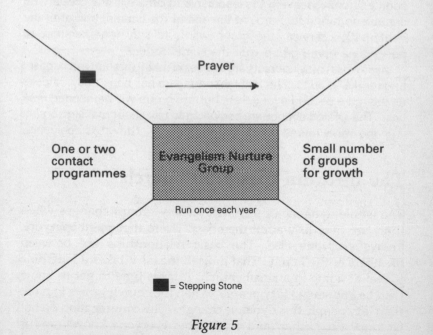

Figure 5

once a month and a crèche every Sunday for the under-threes. A toddler group is started by two young Christian mums, backed up by a number of retired people in the church. The vicar (who has three other small churches in his care) puts his energy initially into training and enabling a baptism preparation team. A church in the city, fifteen miles away, runs a training programme for faith-sharing with people in the home, and five people from St James are able to go and be trained.

Over the next six months this team conducts a series of visits to about half a dozen couples and two or three single people, contacted mainly through baptisms and the toddler group. All the new Christians are drawn together, with some who are still enquirers and three or four established church members, to form an evangelism nurture group. The group meets for eight months leading up to a confirmation service. Much is learned and shared and deep relationships are formed. The group is led initially by the vicar. He soon withdraws leaving the leadership to others in the group who are able to take it forward. At the end of the course, and after the confirmation service, the group wants to stay together and so becomes a home group with the same leaders.

Meanwhile, new contacts are still being made through the baptism and toddler groups. The faith-sharing team has been busy. It looks as though a second evangelism nurture group will be needed next year. The church council are beginning to talk about making contact with the newly retired people in the village . . . Growth is beginning.

The medium (pastoral) church

The whole dynamic of a church (or any group) changes when there are over fifty adult members. Up to that point everyone knows everyone else. The basic relationships are between members of the family. That in itself means it takes a long time to feel at home in a small church: it takes time to get to know (and be known by) fifty people. When the church grows to more than fifty people this dynamic changes. The congregation do not all know each other (and cannot) but everyone knows (and is known by) the pastor, who will normally be full-time and able to focus on one congregation.

It is well worth saying that making the transition between a small and medium church, between medium and large, and large to very large can be a difficult time for both congregation and ministers. There is a "letting go" at each stage of the process: by the minister and by the congregation. It can be especially hard for the congregation and lay leaders in a small church to let go of the need to know everyone else in the family and to allow the church to grow beyond a certain size. It is also hard for those who have been central in leadership for many years in the small church situation to hand over the reins to the minister for the next part of the journey. Unless that happens, however, it is hard for growth to continue.

Although there are difficulties in transition, there is great potential. At this point in the life of the church growth can happen quite quickly but will depend to a large extent on the role and ministry of the vicar or pastor. It is the pastor who gives the church its cohesiveness and support. There will normally be a high expectation – caught by new people as well – that the clergy person will be there when he or she is needed. The increased numbers in church mean that more people can be involved in contact ministries and in the stepping stone evangelism.

In this size of church it may well be best for the pastor to lead the evangelism nurture group, providing his gifts are suited to the task. If he is unable to lead the group himself then he should play a very active role within it. The pastor's leadership of this group means that strong relationships will be formed between himself and each new member of the church. Good pastoral care is provided, some assessment of gifts and abilities can be made, and new Christians can be established in ministry very soon. Although the pastor will be leading, it's still important that more established Christians are included in the groups as members and as co-leaders.

Leading a church at this stage in its growth is not easy, especially as the numbers in the congregation approach 150. Work and expectations increase as the congregation grows. If the growth happens rapidly considerable strain can be placed on the established Christians within the congregation. It is vital at this stage that the pastor is spending time building up the lay leadership, which will become increasingly important as the church continues to grow.

FEATURES OF AN EVANGELISM NURTURE GROUP IN A MEDIUM CHURCH
1. Most people will join the church and the group through some contact with the pastor
2. Providing contact structures are in place, groups can be run continuously through the year
3. If many people are joining through one of the stepping stones the course can start further forward in the faith
4. The pastor either needs to lead the group himself or be very closely involved in its life
5. Its still important that established church members should take part as co-leaders
6. At the end of the course the group can continue as a home group or members may join existing home groups in threes or fours

Two years on St James' is still growing. The diocese, which thinks strategically, has agreed to the clergy team being expanded. A deacon has come and taken pastoral charge at St James' leaving the vicar free to work with the other churches in the group, which are still struggling. About seventy adults now come to church on a Sunday. Good contacts were established with the newly retired who had moved into the village. It turned out that several had been active church members many years previously. They joined an evangelism nurture group, together with one or two more young mums, and that group too is continuing to meet as a home group now.

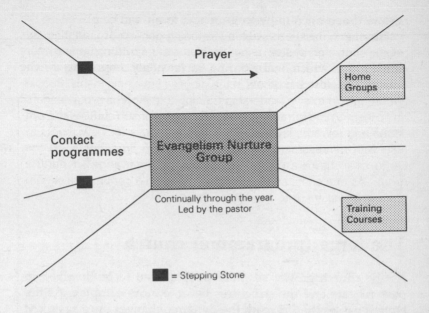

Figure 6

All of these new people in the church mean that there is more time and energy for the routine tasks of the church's life. Jayne, the new deacon, finds that most of the on-going administrative tasks can be handed on to others. She is able to spend her time visiting contacts on the fringe of the church. There are still very few men in the congregation and the church looks for some way to make contact there. Sports evenings in the church hall are suggested and a new programme is begun.

Jayne finds that quite soon after arriving there are enough people ready to begin an evangelism nurture group. She finds co-leaders and the group begins — it runs for about fifteen weeks. Whilst that group is running, new contacts emerge and a new group is all set to begin as soon as the old one comes to an end. People from the first group have gone to join the existing home groups. It looks as though the second group has a natural cohesion and so Jayne plans to form a new home group from the evangelism nurture group once the course comes to an end.

The church passes through a stretching period now. All the new people bring a great deal of joy. Problems of growth come one after another. The stress on Jayne, particularly, becomes greater and greater. The vicar and others in the diocese are a help in this. People are brought in to give leadership training to the home group leaders and others so the burden of pastoral care begins to shift away from Jayne and towards lay leaders. There are ideas for new teams to help with bereavement visiting and marriage preparation. At the centre of all the life and growth, however, is the evangelism nurture group. As one ends, another begins, bringing a continuous stream of new Christians into the life of the church.

The large (programme) church

As the church grows, so more people need to be involved in pastoral care and the structures become more complex. As the church passes the 150 mark the dynamic changes once again. At this stage no one can know everyone within the congregation in a meaningful way, even the full-time pastor. This means that people do not find their place and welcome by relating to the pastor any more but by becoming part of a part of the church, usually a small group or organization.

This size of church is characterized most by programmes looking after different areas of the church's life, headed up by different teams of people.

A large church is able to mount a wide and increasing variety of contact programmes. If the structures are working well these may well produce too many interested contacts to be fed into just one evangelism nurture group led by the pastor. Whereas at an earlier stage the pastor's involvement in leading the group is the key to the church moving forward, at this stage in the church's growth others need to be involved. If the pastor does all of the evangelism nurture himself then he or she will become the constraint to growth. The vicar or church leader still needs to be involved at some point: whether teaching some of the groups;

or teaching part of each group; certainly in teaching and training the leaders and planning the programme.

In this size of church growth programmes will be diverse. For many churches the basic unit of pastoral care and learning will be the home group, but this may well be supplemented by a variety of training conferences and courses within and outside the congregation. Christians from other churches and traditions may by now be attracted into what is becoming a large church. Generally speaking, it is important that Christians who transfer into the church take part in some way in the evangelism nurture groups so that they have a full understanding of what this church believes and teaches new Christians, and so that they themselves can soon find a place within the life and ministry of their new congregation.

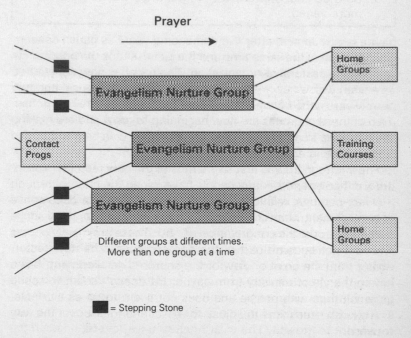

Figure 7

FEATURES OF AN EVANGELISM NURTURE GROUP IN A LARGE CHURCH

1. Several groups may be running at once, with new groups starting every term.

2. The senior leader cannot lead all the groups himself. Other leaders need to be trained in the task.

3. The senior leader should remain involved: either leading some groups or leading part of each group.

4. Christians moving into the church from outside should be encouraged to take part in the groups.

5. Both contact and growth programmes will be much more varied.

Jayne left St James' after five demanding years as parish deacon. The vicar left at the same time and the diocese took the opportunity to do some pastoral re-organization. The parish is now constituted as a team with a new team rector and curate at St James' and two team vicars, who between them care for the other three churches. Two of these churches are now beginning to grow and are making the transition from family to pastoral churches, with help and advice from the congregation at St James'.

The interregnum and first six months of the new rector's ministry are a difficult period. Many people have joined the church through a close, personal relationship with Jayne. There is a deep sense of bereavement when she leaves. As many as twenty or thirty adults drift away out of the congregation of 150. These are mainly people who did not become part of the home groups. The new rector, rightly from the point of view of the church's development, has a different style of ministry from Jayne. He doesn't seem to spend as much time with people and does not seem to be as available. The church needs time to adjust; to reflect and to discover the way forward.

During this period lay leadership emerges. A time of renewal and re-commitment follows. The church takes the opportunity, with outside help, to conduct a mission audit: to catch God's vision for the future and to plan for growth. Many of the original contact programmes have now wound down or run out of energy. Some of these are closed; others receive new leaders; new contact ventures begin. New life is breathed into the stepping stones evangelism as the curate takes charge of this area of work throughout the team. The rector, working with a small group, revises and renews the evangelism nurture group programme. The course if revised and re-written and becomes the basis for a home group course initially, having been taught to the leaders. There is an increased emphasis in the course now on commitment, on giving, on fellowship and on ministry. Once this has been done, the first groups are offered to enquirers and new Christians. The rector leads these himself to begin with, as Jayne did. As the contact programmes develop several groups are needed at once. Daytime sessions develop alongside evening groups. Lay people who have the right gifts and abilities emerge and are trained to lead the groups. Short-term enquirers groups begin, aimed at different age and social groups, and in time become nurture groups themselves.

After an initial period of transition a structure emerges where all of the groups are lay led with the rector or curate teaching three sessions of each course toward the end of the group's life. As at the pastoral stage, some of the groups go on to become home groups. Others divide, with the new Christians joining established home groups in twos and threes.

Home groups in St James' have now become fortnightly not weekly, giving those involved time and space for ministry as well as being committed to fellowship. Many of the people who are becoming Christians have very little knowledge of the faith. Courses are offered regularly, through the church's training centre, on understanding the Bible, on prayer and many other aspects of the Christian life, to back up and support what is happening in the evangelism nurture programme and the home groups.

While all this has been taking place there has been a need to improve and extend the church plant, and the church will soon come to the point where it needs to face the challenge of increasing the full-time staff. Simultaneously the challenge for the leaders is to go on catching and communicating a vision for the next stage of the church's life.

Although the structures and programmes have become more complex now, the fourfold pattern is the same: contact, evangelism, nurture, growth. Within this size of church the focus will gradually move towards the growth programmes, which will need more creative thinking by the staff team. However, the evangelism nurture groups are still the cornerstone of all that happens later. A strong foundation is being laid for Christian lives: the course itself defines what this church believes in many different fundamentals of faith; through the different groups people are being brought to faith, established in fellowship and beginning in ministry.

The extra-large (corporation) church

Although the structures of a programme church are complex (and continually changing) there is a strong sense throughout the community of belonging to a whole; of all being part of the same family. You may not know everyone else in the church but there is a network of friendship and fellowship across the whole which binds the community together. Once a certain size is reached (around 350) this dynamic changes again. At this point the church itself needs to subdivide in one way or another. Henceforth people find their sense of belonging to the community from being part of a small group and a larger sub-church, as well as being part of the church as a whole structure.

This division can take place in a number of ways. It can happen through church planting: sixty or so church members with an established leader plant a church elsewhere in the parish or locality, which remains part of the church as a whole but develops its own life as well. It can take place through dividing congregations. This may already have happened in terms of main services, depending on the size of the building. There is a difference, however, between dividing a congregation because of size and because of structure. Where the division is based on size, although there may be two main morning services, all the other structures function as they did before (contact programmes, evangelism nurture groups, home groups, etc.), drawing on the whole church for membership. Where this develops into a structural division each congregation will have its own leadership, pastoral care, contact and nurture programmes, etc.

The third way division can take place is through age/gender/ interest groups. This form of structural division doesn't affect the way the congregation worships (whether in one service or three, depending on the size of the building). But all of the structural divisions are according to age and status. There will be, for example, an extensive children's and youth programme, with a staff member in charge and its own evangelism nurture structure;

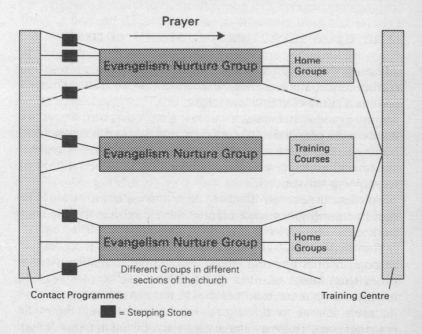

Figure 8

a young adults and a retired persons programme with similar structures in place. This third way of dividing will work best in a large, city-centre church not tied to residential areas. For most situations one of the first two divisions will be preferable.

The evangelism nurture groups function in the extra large church much as in the pastoral or programme churches, depending on how the division works. However the dividing happens, in effect the extra large church is a number of smaller churches combined: a programme church with several pastoral or family churches within one structure.

Five years on again and St James' is continuing to grow, together with other churches in the team parish. In fact, St James' didn't wait until it reached 350 adults before deciding to divide. The building, even after refurbishment, was getting cramped when the congregation reached 225 adults. Instead of dividing the services, which would have been one option, the church decided to plant a new congregation in a neighbouring area – a new housing estate where there was no centre of worship. Sixty adult members of the church came forward to begin the new congregation with the existing curate. The plant has established itself and is beginning to grow as a pastoral church two years on.

It took time for St James' to recover from losing so many active members but people are still coming in and the church is beginning to grow again. There is no staff member available at the present time to lead a plant and so the church is now considering dividing the morning service.

The team increasingly functions as a whole group. The fact that the same evangelism nurture programme is used in all the churches in the team gives a common sense of identity and Christian calling. Two small Methodist churches have joined the team as well, to create a Local Ecumenical Project, adding the Methodist minister to the team structure. Two of the other churches are working through the transition from pastoral to programme churches. One of these is actively considering a plant. Four times a year the whole group get together for a large-scale celebration in the local leisure centre.

The evangelism nurture course is the same across all the churches and church plants across the group. In some churches the staff lead the groups, in others they are lay led. Twice a year all involved in the programme meet to plan, pray and reflect. Changes in the course are made on a regular basis at these meetings.

The church has come a long way in the twenty years of its growth. There have been ups and downs and many difficulties on the way. The structures have needed to change at each stage of the journey. The prayer has remained constant and is the single biggest reason for the growth. Even so at this stage in St James's life, less than twenty per cent of the people in the parish are Christians, leaving eighty per cent who are not. Groups for evangelism and nurture have remained a cornerstone of the growth through the whole of that period, although their role within the structure has changed as the church has grown.

Real life, of course, is never so simple as the story of St James'. In reality, more major problems may well have occurred to inhibit growth: the organist and choir may have left to join a house church; the churchwarden has an affair with a home group leader; the bishop is opposed to growth rather than supporting it and refuses to increase the staff in any way; the PCC members simply refuse to change. All these problems, and countless others, can and will occur. There is a way through each one of them. As the church prays and moves forward it is as though the river of the Holy Spirit's life flows deeper and wider (Ezekiel 47). When any rising river meets obstacles, such as a rock or a fallen tree, the flow may be delayed or altered in some small way but the rising river always finds its own course around whatever is in the way. Growth can happen in every different size of church and evangelism nurture groups will play a vital role.

Note to chapter 4

1. Arlin Rothauge, *Sizing up a Congregation for New Member Ministry* (New York: The Episcopal Church Center).

5

Culture and liturgy

Local culture and the group

Take three parishes in the same diocese: one in a run-down council estate where there are racial tensions; one in the smartest part of a small town with large detached houses; one in a small rural community ten miles from the nearest Sainsbury's. The culture of each area will be very different. It would be foolish to attempt to run a group for evangelism and nurture in the same way in each of these parishes. The social context must affect the life of the group.

There are five questions about your own context which need to be thought through in planning groups for evangelism nurture. Many parishes contain several different communities, each with their own culture. So long as the church is small all of these communities will need to be served by the same group. As more resources become available it may be possible to offer several different styles of group within the same parish.

FIVE QUESTIONS ABOUT SOCIAL CONTEXT

1. **Are people willing to come out for meetings?**
   If the answer is "yes", there is no problem. If it is "no" (whether through fear of crime or because it just doesn't happen) this needs to be thought through. Transport to and from meetings may need to be arranged. Sometimes people who are economically poor find it hard to go to the house of someone who is well-off and vice versa. Neutral ground, such as a church lounge or vicarage, can be easier.

---

2. **Is the culture a "book" culture?**
   This will affect the material you use in the group and
   the way it is presented and taught. If most of the
   potential group have not read a non-fiction book
   since they left school it is not wise to depend too
   much on a book for your course, or on them doing
   back-up reading. People will need to be introduced
   very gently to the idea of Bible reading, especially in
   public. Simple videos may be helpful, instead of long
   talks. One of the things which makes people very
   hesitant in coming to groups is a fear of sharing their
   ignorance and being embarrassed in front of others.
   Most of your group will just naturally assume that
   everyone else knows far more than they do. Even an
   environment full of books can be off-putting for
   many. Special care needs to be taken with adults
   who cannot read at all.

3. **Are there any obvious tensions in the community?**
   There may be tensions between black and white;
   between council estate and other parts of the
   community; between young and old; between "in-
   comer" and established residents of a village. All of
   these tensions will be brought into the life of the
   group; as the group grows they will need to be
   addressed.

4. **Are people used to talking with strangers?**
   Some of us are. If you are a clergyperson, a teacher
   or a solicitor the chances are you are used to talking
   to people you don't know. The thought of being in a
   room full of strangers holds little fear for you. But
   the same room and same people can be terrifying for
   the person who is unused to such things, or who
   has been badly hurt in the past and feels vulnerable
   now.

5. **Are there any special groups in the community?**
   Different cultures require different measures. In some
   cultures men find it hard to join mixed groups. In

some places many women find it hard to come out
at night, either because they are working or because
their husbands won't let them come to church
groups. The elderly can be a special group when it
comes to nurture. So can young marrieds. The
opportunities and the challenges are very many.

The following story shows the wrong way, and then the right
way, to establish an evangelism nurture group, taking culture into
account. See if you can spot the differences and the mistakes.

Nigel and Rose are both teachers, recent college graduates and
members of St Whatnot's church in a slightly run-down (but not
desperate) area of town. Both are committed Christians and have
joined the church fresh from their experience of college Christian
Unions. The vicar, who is very pleased to have them, invites Nigel
and Rose to run an evangelism nurture group. He's under pressure
so there isn't much time to plan and prepare. Nigel and Rose are
left to choose their own material and are simply given a list of
''likely'' people.

The couple send typed invitations to the twenty people on the
list, inviting them to come to the first meeting at their flat at 8.00
p.m. in three weeks' time. On the relevant evening they put out
twenty chairs, provide a light supper for twenty and are a little bit
embarrassed when only five people turn up. Nigel opens the group
in prayer and asks people to say who they are and why they have
come. Rose plays the guitar and there is a half-hearted attempt to
sing. Then everyone is asked to turn to Luke 15:11 in their Bible
and to read aloud, in turn, a few verses from the passage. Nigel
throws in a few questions for the group to discuss. Some have
painfully obvious answers (''What did the younger son do when
his money ran out?''). Some are a bit obscure (''What does the
famine in the land tell us about the economic climate today?''). Nigel
and Rose smile a lot but there are some awkward silences. It was
never like this at the college CU. Then they show part of the video
with several famous Christian speakers who talk about the Christian
life. Rose ends the meeting by leading a time of prayer in which

Rose prays aloud, then Nigel, then Nigel again, then Rose. Coffee is served and people leave around ten. There is no contact with the group midweek. Only two people return the following Wednesday. Shortly afterwards the group dies.

Dorothy, in her mid-fifties, was quite pleased to receive an invitation to the new group. She was widowed recently and had started coming to church. It took her a while to work out what it was all about. She'd never heard of a ''basics group'' and had no idea what it did. The only typed letters she normally received were from her bank manager. She was very lonely, though, and decided to give it a try. Perhaps this was the way to make friends. She asked the vicar for directions to the flat. He seemed pleased she was going and introduced her to Rose, who was nice but very young.

Dorothy left home very early to walk to the group meeting, frightened of being late. She had a fifteen minute walk (it was still daylight, just). She arrived twenty minutes early and spent time looking in shop windows, resisting the temptation to bolt for home. Operating the entry phone to the flats was hard, so was knocking on Nigel and Rose's front door. When Dorothy saw all the chairs it was a relief to know that a lot of people were coming. As the minutes ticked by the chairs became more and more of an embarrassment. There was some attempt at conversation but not much. Dorothy felt awkward and began to wish she hadn't come. The flat was the poshest she'd ever seen; full of paintings and lined with books. All these people here must be very clever . . .

Dorothy found it hard to make friends but had just begun to talk to a nice lady on her left when Nigel interrupted and said a prayer. They passed round a kind of hymn book next and the lady got out her guitar. ''That's nice,'' thought Dorothy. ''She's going to sing . . . Oh my word, they want us all to join in.''

Worse was to follow. Everyone was asked to turn to Luke 15 in their Bibles. Dorothy had to own up to not having a Bible (she was given one). She had no idea where (or what) Luke's gospel was and got in a flummox with the pages. Then everyone was asked to read aloud. Dorothy hadn't read anything aloud since her children

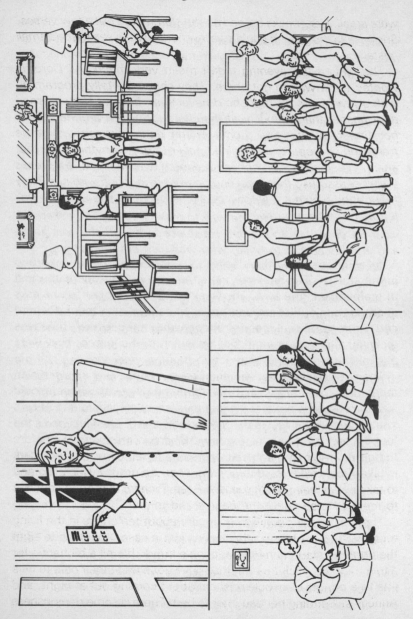

*were small. Her cheeks burned as she stammered out a few verses.
She wished the ground could swallow her up when she made a small
mistake.*

*The rest of the evening didn't mean very much. All Dorothy
wanted to do was to get home. They showed a telly programme
with a few vicars on that she'd never seen before. They seemed
a lot posher than the vicar at the church. She left around ten for
her fifteen-minute walk home in the dark. She arrived home
trembling and upset, determined never to go to anything like that
again. When she didn't appear at church over the next few weeks
the vicar assumed that Nigel and Rose were in touch with her. They
thought he would go. Neither had time to check and Dorothy was
left alone in her sorrow . . .*

Nigel and Rose have offered to lead a new evangelism nurture group
in the church. They are very gifted but are out of tune with most
of the people in the area. The vicar accepts their offer but he asks
another couple, Richard and Anne, to co-lead with them. Richard
and Anne are local people and have both become Christians
recently, after they brought their daughter to be baptized. They were
part of the last adult confirmation group a year ago.

The two couples meet with the vicar over three evenings and plan
the course in great detail. They agree that Nigel and Rose should
lead the meetings but that the group will meet at Richard and Anne's
house: people will feel more comfortable there. The vicar gives the
four leaders a list and the team work hard in the six weeks before
the group begins visiting each person on their own territory. Care
is taken to explain to each person what the group will be like and
to take away their fears. Nigel and Rose, Richard and Anne continue
to meet to pray about the course and to plan.

The first evening arrives. There are about ten chairs in the living
room, with some more in the kitchen just in case. About ten to eight
the doorbell starts ringing and people arrive. It's all a bit hectic for
a few minutes. Richard and Rose have gone off in their cars to give
lifts to a couple of people hesitant about coming out at night, and
Anne is still putting her daughter to bed. There is some nervousness

as people are introduced but general amazement as the room begins to fill up and fifteen people are packed in.

Nigel begins the evening by welcoming everyone and suggesting everyone takes a couple of minutes to talk to their neighbour about who they are and why they've come. There's no shortage of things to say. Everyone takes it in turns to introduce their partner to the group. After that people are far more relaxed. Nigel gives some input. Richard and Anne tell the story of how they became Christians. There's some more discussion in groups and a time to ask questions. In no time it's half past nine. Nigel and Richard make the coffee and pass round the biscuits. Nobody seems to want to go home. Transport is arranged for those without cars, both for a lift home and for next week, so no one has to walk. Nigel and Rose liaise with Richard and Anne after the meeting to review what has happened. During the week they arrange to contact each member of the group to check everything was OK and also to contact the five who didn't come. The group is under way . . .

Dorothy is surprised, but pleased, when Anne and Rose call round to invite her to the new group starting at Anne's house. Dorothy has known Richard and Anne by sight for years. She's hesitant about going at first (it's not easy meeting strangers) but going to church has been the only good thing to happen to her since Stan died and it would be good to get to know people better. She decides to make the effort and is relieved to know that Rose will pick her up in the car at 7.45.

Even so, Dorothy is nervous and ready in good time. It's much easier arriving with someone else. Richard and Anne's house is very nice, like hers when she was younger. There are one or two familiar faces there from church and everyone is soon chatting. Dorothy finds herself next to Sue, a young mum. During the opening exercise she finds herself telling Sue all about Stan and his last illness, and all the things that have happened. It's a relief to talk. It seems a bit nerve-racking to have to introduce Sue to the group but everyone else is nervous too. Most people are just like her: wanting to get more involved; wanting to learn more, but nervous at the same time.

Richard and Anne's story is really interesting. Fancy a plumber becoming a Christian! Everything that's said makes her think. There's no shortage of things to ask or talk about and Dorothy is quite reluctant to leave at ten o'clock. She arrives home feeling a lot lighter than when she went: like a burden has been lifted.

Anne pops in a few days later just to see how Dorothy got on, which is nice. It's a chance to talk through a few things Dorothy didn't understand and to ask Anne some questions she didn't dare ask on the night. Dorothy was afraid since the meeting that she was too quiet but Anne is able to reassure her on this. They agree to see each other on Sunday at church and Dorothy finds herself looking forward to each of the group meetings as they come round . . .

God is the great bridge-builder. The Gospel is able to cross cultural barriers of all kinds. We need to recognize that those barriers are there in every parish and every situation. We need to think imaginatively about possible problems and how to overcome them. We need to look at things honestly from the point of view of the person coming to a group. It makes a difference.

Christian nurture and confirmation

All that is happening in an evangelism nurture group has to be related at some point (or points) to the wider life of the church, locally and beyond. This will happen most often through special services of church membership. In the Church of England this mean baptism and confirmation.

Every church must tackle the question of how structures and groups for evangelism and nurture are to relate to adult baptism and confirmation services. There are three different models, broadly speaking. Whichever one is adopted will depend on the tradition of the local church and the theological position of the church leaders. My own preference is for the third.

Growing New Christians

The "confirmation class"

Each year at St Columba's there is a confirmation service. The bishop comes either to that church or to another nearby. Four months before the vicar announces the forthcoming event and draws a group of adults and a group of children together. The course of instruction about the Christian life is geared towards the end-point and high-point of the confirmation service. At the service itself members of the group are received into membership of the church through baptism and/or confirmation.

This is the model which has operated in thousands of Anglican parishes for many years. It has serious weaknesses, outlined below.

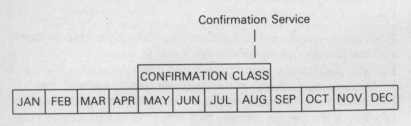

Figure 9

Confirmation classes do have the merit of being familiar within most Anglican parishes (although most outsiders have no idea what they are). Largely speaking, however, the model needs to be changed. If your own church is entrenched in this model and cannot as yet break free of it, these changes may be a first stage.

WEAKNESSES IN THE CONFIRMATION CLASS MODEL

1. **Groups for evangelism nurture can only be run once a year in the run up to the confirmation.** This restricts growth. It is nonsense for a church's whole strategy for evangelism and nurture to be geared to the availability of the bishop.

2. **Tying the group to the confirmation service affects the timing of the course.** The way bishops have to plan their diaries means that the confirmation will be at a different time of year each year (February in 1993, September in 1994 and so on). These months may be more or less convenient for running an evangelism nurture group.

3. **The whole emphasis of the group inevitably becomes preparing for confirmation; for the service.** Learning about living the Christian life becomes a secondary, sometimes incidental part of the programme leading up to the "big day". People come on the course not to learn about the Christian faith but so they can be confirmed.

4. **The confirmation service is wrongly seen as some kind of "graduation ceremony" for adults as well as children.** The danger is that people feel they are graduating out of the need to go on learning and meeting with other Christians.

5. **The model takes no note of the fact that people are at many different stages of their journey within one group.** Not everyone will be ready to be confirmed at the same time.

6. **The model (and the name of the group) takes no account of the mix of appropriate liturgical responses to people's varied spiritual experience.** Within any one group this will include confirmation (after baptism as an infant); baptism by full immersion followed at a later date by confirmation; baptism and confirmation at the same service; being received into the Church of England from another episcopal denomination; the renewal of baptismal promises; or no liturgical response at all.

7. **The model severely limits those who feel eligible to take part in the group.** Very tentative enquirers may be put off because they know they are not ready to be confirmed. Those who have actually been confirmed in the past, but have drifted away, will be prevented from coming because they have no need of confirmation (but have a great need for a simple course of instruction in the Christian faith).

DEVELOPING A CONFIRMATION CLASS MODEL
1. **Change the name of the group.** Make the name broader than "Confirmation Class" and more meaningful to outsiders. "Class" brings to mind school: rows of desks; a teacher at the front; people taking notes; exams. These are negative images for many people. "Confirmation" is simply a mystery word to those outside the church.
2. **Stress with every invitation that everyone and anyone is welcome.** Specifically include those who are just enquirers at present as well as those who have been confirmed in the past and would like a "refresher".
3. **Continue the course for at least four to six weeks after the confirmation service.** You want to communicate the need to go on growing and learning beyond the confirmation itself. Plan for the group to go on growing in some way.

The catechumenate

The early church, at a certain period of its history, had a very developed programme of Christian initiation called the catechumenate (a catechumen was simply a learner, one receiving instruction). The person being initiated passed through a series of stages. Each transition from one stage to another was marked by a specific liturgy and often took place at a particular time of year. The overall process from beginning to end took many months.

The idea of the adult catechumenate has been revived in recent years. It began in the Roman Catholic Church in a significant way with the Second Vatican Council. The scheme is well-developed within the Roman Catholic Church in Britain (called "The Rite for the Christian Initiation of Adults" – RCIA[1]) and is increasingly finding its way into the Church of England.[2] The catechumenate movement contains many powerful and helpful insights about adult Christian nurture, not least the idea of a person being on a journey into faith.

There is no standard model for the catechumenate in the Church of England and much variety still in the Roman Catholic Church. In the sense of being modelled on a journey, the whole approach outlined here could be said to be based on the catechumenate. However, one of the distinctive features of the more developed catechumenate approach is the way that different points on the journey are marked in the church's liturgy and the church's year.

The whole process of the catechumenate is not easily understood in a day's study, let alone in a few paragraphs. However, for the sake of those who would like to know a little so that they can learn more, the four main stages of the process are outlined below:

1. *Enquiry and Welcome (the pre-catechumenate)*
A group of enquirers is formed from within the congregation. Each enquirer has one or more sponsors to help them along the journey. The group comes together over several weeks. There is a strong emphasis on welcome and telling one's story. An agenda for the next stage of the process is sometimes drawn together. People are able to opt out at the end of this or any of the other stages. In the developed RCIA model this pre-catechumenate takes place in Advent.

2. *The Instruction Stage (the catechumenate)*
At Christmas or Epiphany those who have been enquirers take part in the Celebration of the Rite of Enrolment before the congregation. The whole congregation takes a responsibility for those who are learning about the Way. Sponsors continue in the group for a period of instruction and learning. The length of this instruction period varies. If the process is compressed into one liturgical cycle it will last through Epiphany to the first or second Sunday in Lent, but may last for much longer.

3. *Deeper Spiritual Preparation (illumination)*
The whole church celebrates the Rite of Election of catechumens as those who have been part of the group so far make their

decision to be baptized and/or confirmed. In the Roman Catholic church this is often a diocesan service. Space is given in Lent for going deeper as part of the ongoing life of the church – often there will be no specific preparation group in this period. At Easter the catechumens are received into full membership of the church through baptism and or confirmation and receive Holy Communion for the first time.

4. *Deepening of Faith (mystagogia)*
The group remains together for a short period of time, either from Easter to Pentecost or in the weeks after Pentecost. During this time further issues relating to living out the faith are explored.

The Catechumenate Model

Rite of Enrolment		Rite of Election	Baptism								
1	2		3	4							
DEC	JAN	FEB	MAR	APR	MAY	JUN	JUL	AUG	SEP	OCT	NOV

1. Pre-catechumenate
2. Catechumante
3. Illumination
4. Going deeper

Figure 10

Without a doubt there are many good things for Christians of all traditions to learn from the emerging catechumenate movement. There is a richness within our common tradition which is well worth exploring. If that common tradition also helps us to work more closely across the denominations, so much the better. I have particularly appreciated the catechumenate movements emphasis on the idea of faith as journey; and on the involvement of the whole congregation in the process of initiation both at a liturgical level and through sponsors.

However, there are three questions which need to be asked of the catechumenate as a whole and asked by any church looking to develop a model along these lines:

1. *Is it flexible?*

We are in a mission situation. A mission situation calls for great flexibility. Whatever groups or structures we devise for drawing people to faith will always remain a means to an end, not an end in themselves. A group which is helpful is better than any number of neat systems. Theologically and liturgically the catechumenate is geared to those who are outside the church and who are not baptized. But the reality of our mission situation is that most adults returning to faith are already baptized. Many were confirmed as children. A structure for initiation which is closely geared to preparation for baptism is going to exclude a very large number of enquirers in the same way as the confirmation class model.

The same lack of flexibility in timing groups and courses is here with this model as with the traditional confirmation class. Enquirers' courses can begin only at one place in the year. For small churches this may be enough for reasons of resources. But larger churches will want to be starting off different groups at different times whenever possible. If a person begins to come to church in May, they may stay around as part of the worshipping family until November before becoming part of a group. On the other hand they may get fed up with not knowing anyone in the church and with not really understanding what the faith is about, and they may begin to look elsewhere for the answers they are seeking. The time of spiritual harvest will not always correspond with the cycle of our Christian year.

The third need for flexibility is that different people move along their journey at different rates. There really are very sudden, swift conversions. Others are much slower and more steady. Can a four-stage process really serve the needs of both groups and those in between?

2. *Is it simple?*

If we are serious about being in a mission situation then the whole of our approach to those who are enquirers needs to be simple and straightforward – user-friendly is the jargon. We need to be pointing people to the Lord, not to ourselves. The rhythm of the church's year seems so natural to those of us who are on the inside. But to the average person in society it means nothing at all. Christmas and Easter perhaps mean something – but Advent, Lent and Epiphany? The language of the four-stage catechumenate is complex. Even where the language has been simplified, the ideas are hard to grasp: if clergy and lay leaders have trouble with them how will the outsider fare?

Most explorations of the catechumenate I have come across assume that the initial group of enquirers will come from within the wider church family – those who are already worshippers. How effective is the catechumenate in drawing in those who are not yet regular worshippers but who would like to learn more? For those who are unchurched newcomers to the faith being confirmed can be a very big thing: to have to take them through two additional rites as well seems unnecessary and unhelpful – especially if by that time they are ready and wanting to be baptized or confirmed.

3. *Is there enough teaching?*

Those who have been developing the catechumenate are to some extent reacting against old, rigid ways of teaching the faith which have not worked for them, or for many others. For this reason there is a very low emphasis in much of the catechumenate material on syllabus, programme and teaching input. There is a very high emphasis on mutual sharing and on discovering the faith that is already within you. Perhaps this emphasis is right in certain situations but, for those who have very little understanding of faith or gospel, clear teaching is needed too.

An on-going nurture programme

The third model makes only a minimum link between groups for evangelism and nurture and public liturgy. In a growing church evangelism nurture groups need to be offered at all times of the year, in different contexts, to all kinds of people (including enquirers, new Christians, established church members, those returning after drifting away). The work of these groups will be such an important part of a church that those planning the groups need to be free from the constraints of fitting in with particular services or special times of the year. In a mission situation, the greatest need with all of these groups is to be flexible and adaptable, not tied to times and seasons which may mean a great deal to those on the inside but nothing at all to the majority without.

Moreover, the members of these groups need to be free to decide when and what kind of liturgical expression is appropriate for them, and at what stage of their journey. To tie the groups in to a one-off programme or special service is simply too restrictive. Nor should it be our priority to immerse new Christians in a completely foreign and alien culture of church. Structures and services need to be simple so they can be communicated simply to those who are still outside.

The model we adopt is to run evangelism nurture groups throughout the year, as they are needed and as we have the resources. There is little to be gained in our situation by having liturgies and services of admission for the different stages of initiation. Becoming a Christian is not a complicated thing and we have no right to make it so.

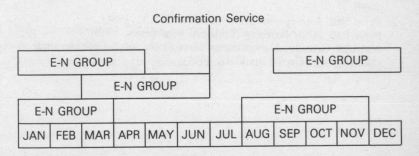

Figure 11

Within that framework of on-going groups the opportunity for

confirmation comes once a year, at different times of the year.
At that point all those who have been through Christians for Life
groups in the previous year are invited to take part in the service
in an appropriate way: to be baptized; confirmed; received into
the Church or to renew baptismal vows. All are welcomed into
membership of the church by the bishop and by the whole
congregation. One or two preparatory meetings are held prior
to the service itself, to go through the words of the service and
emphasize their meaning, but the main preparation has already
taken place within the groups.

Handling confirmation in this way does mean that confirmation
needs to be separated from the beginning to receive Holy
Communion. In our own system, once a person has received
instruction about Holy Communion in the Christians for Life
course, providing they are a Christian, they are welcome to begin
to receive Holy Communion and to anticipate their confirmation.
Some choose to wait until they are confirmed but most appreciate
the opportunity to join in fully with the sacraments of the church
and to be part of the family in this respect.

Notes to chapter 5

1. *The Right of Christian Initiation* (London: St Thomas More Centre,
   1988).
2. Peter Ball, *Journey into Faith* (London: SPCK, 1984).
   Peter Ball, *Adult Believing* (London: Mowbrays, 1988).
   Malcolm Grundy, *Evangelization through the Adult Catechumenate*
   (Nottingham: Grove Booklets, 1991).

6

Planning a syllabus

The Church of England has no National Curriculum. There are no guidelines laid down from the centre about what adult Christians should be taught at the outset of their Christian life, other than the catechism. So far as I know, no diocese has made an attempt to do this either. The result is that every man does what is right in his own eyes. The subjects covered in confirmation classes, basics groups and similar ventures vary enormously from church to church.

Everyone would agree that designing a curriculum is a central part of any educational activity. Most of us would say we believe that teaching people to be disciples is the most important and the most privileged area of education of them all. Why do we pay so little attention to the syllabus?

It's worth saying that the Chuch of England's lack of central guidelines has not been followed by other denominations. The Roman Catholic Church, in particular, is many years ahead of the Anglicans in developing programmes of learning, a curriculum and learning tools for teaching adults the basics of faith. The work in the Roman Catholic Church is centrally directed and resourced and not, as in the Church of England, left to independent publishers and home mission groups.

This chapter looks at the important question of the syllabus for an evangelism nurture group. How long should the course be? What should it cover? What is the best order for the topics? How should the material be presented? The aim is not to give you a recommended or ready-made syllabus (although my own is included), but to help you think through the issues and draw up your own.

How long should the course be?

"By the grace God has given to me, I laid a foundation as an expert builder." 1 Corinthians 3:10

How long does it take to lay a foundation of Christian belief which will last the rest of a person's life? which will answer the basic questions we all have? which will give a secure foundation for the future? There is no single right answer. Every situation and every person is different. A lot depends on where people have come to in their journey when they begin the course. Will they still be enquirers or will most of the group already have come to a point of commitment? What are the opportunities for learning and growing once the course has ended? How easily will people take to meeting in groups?

There is a need to balance these factors – the needs of the people in the group – against the needs of the whole church. How many groups are needed over the course of the year? Who are the people best equipped to lead them? Is there a need to fit in with any other programmes or dates in the life of the church or with a termly cycle of events?

The material you want to use may also influence your decision, but shouldn't be the major factor. There are courses which claim to be for Christian nurture but which only last six weeks. Don't be fooled. Effective Christian nurture is next to impossible in that period of time in a small group, even if everything else is running in your favour. After six weeks together a group of people are only just beginning to trust each other. In a group which is working well the amount which is learned and the significance of the sessions should increase steadily as the course proceeds.

Six weeks is too short. Twelve weeks is an acceptable minimum, in a situation where people alrady have some understanding of faith and are going on to another kind of learning and fellowship group. Even in that situation, fifteen weeks is better. In a group which is beginning from scratch and where the majority are still enquirers, and in a situation where there are no ready-made home groups, twenty to twenty-four weeks is better still.

Once you have made a provisional decision about length, write down a list of weeks to give you some idea of the overall structure. It's important right from the beginning to have some idea of where the group is going. Then use the following section to fill in the subjects for each session.

Themes for each session

Your own syllabus

Imagine, for the purpose of this chapter, that you are planning a syllabus for a typical evangelism nurture group: some new Christians, some enquirers, some established Christians who have joined for a refresher. You are planning a course of fifteen session. The course will be the main preparation for confirmation, supplemented by one session for the candidates just before the service.

Look at the following list of subjects. Make a list in the second column of the fifteen you would include in your course in any order. In the third column put the list into the best logical order you can. You are allowed to combine two or more subjects into one session where the subjects overlap, but you need to recognize that this will mean less full treatment for each subject area.

(Chapter continues on p. 102)

Possible Subjects	Your First Fifteen	Your Subjects in Order
Money and giving Sharing your faith		1.
The Ten Commandments The Lord's Prayer Listening to God		2.
Reading the Bible Bible background and history		3.
The ministry of Jesus The death of Jesus The resurrection of Jesus		4.
The existence of God The Holy Spirit		5.
The gifts of the Holy Spirit The Trinity Baptism		6.
Confirmation Holy Communion Worship		7.
Christian living Fellowship		8.
The Church Becoming a Christian Growing in relationships		9.
Christians at work The problem of suffering Science and faith		10.
Christian hope Ministry		11.
Personal prayer Praying with others Obedience		12.
Going on growing Forgiveness Care for the poor		13.
Other religions Christian assurance Spiritual warfare		14.
(Add your own subjects *not covered in this list)*		15.

Now compare your own syllabus with some published examples given below.

Some published examples

These are ideas for comparison. Full details of the sources are given in the resources section. The authors' own titles for the subjects are given – in most cases these are self-explanatory.

Caring for New Christians[1]	Discovery Groups[2]
1. Believing 2. Being sure 3. Growing 4. Being obedient 5. Being established 6. Continuing	1. Laying foundations 2. The heart of the matter - Jesus 3. Christian Assurance 4. Reading the Bible 5. Learning to pray 6. The Holy Spirit 7. Christian Fellowship 8. Defeating evil 9. Serving Christ
Discipleship Course[3]	**To be Confirmed[4]**
1. How can I know? 2. How can I grow? 3. How can I show? 4. How can I overcome? 5. What can we know about God? 6. Who is Jesus Christ? 7. Who is the Holy Spirit? 8. Is the Bible the Word of God? 9. Why the cross? 10. Prayer 11. Is there life after death? 12. The Church 13. Common questions 14. Giving 15. Guidance 16. Faith 17. Suffering	1. To be confirmed . . . 2. The man who was different 3. Life with the Father 4. The rebel race 5. The death that brought New Life 6. The defeat of death 7. His people filled with his Spirit 8. Out of the old – into the new (conversion-baptism) 9. Living the new life 10. The family together 11. Out in the big wide world 12. The ever open line 13. God's reference library Appendix: The Ten Commandments

Discipleship Course
18. Forgiveness
19. Love
20. Worship
21. The gifts of the Spirit
22. Being filled with the Spirit
23. Spiritual Warfare

Finding Faith[5]
1. The big questions
2. Enter Jesus
3. The heart of the matter
4. God's chosen rabble
5. Read all about it
6. Power for life
7. The other side (sin, suffering, other faiths)
8. The shape of things to come
9. A faith for adults

The Dynamics of Spiritual Growth[6]
1. The dynamics of spiritual growth
2. Hearing God's voice
3. Believing God's word
4. Seeking the Father
5. Submitting to Christ
6. Taking up the cross
7. Depending on the Holy Spirit
8. Fulfilling the great commission

Christian Basics[7]
E1. Jesus: the unique answer
E2. The world: looking beyond science
E3. The Bible: true and relevant
E4. Suffering: why ours? Why God's?
E5. Jesus lives: the bridge to God
E6. The Church: why bother?

N1. A new faith: growing and sharing
N2. A new outlook: a Christian perspective
N3. A new guide: the Bible in daily life
N4. A new responsibility: living as Christ's disciple
N5. A new relationship: discovering prayer

Follow Me[8]

Stage 1 Discovering Jesus
1.1 Who is God
1.2 His Life
1.3 His Ministry
1.4 His Death and Resurrection
1.5 "Do you turn to Christ"

Stage 2 Meeting Jesus
2.1 Seeing Him
2.2 Sharing His Message
2.3 Believing in Him
2.4 Belonging to Him
2.5 Understanding Him

Stage 3 Knowing Jesus
3.1 In Baptism
3.2 The Healer
3.3 The Lamb of God
3.4 The Food of Pilgrims
3.5 In Your Life

Christian Basics
N6. A new family: joining the church

D1. The Christian story: God with us
D2. The Christian story: God at work
D3. The Christian story: recorded in the Bible
D4. The Christian story: centred on the cross
D5. The Christian story: taking our part
D6. The Christian story: continuing in the church

I1. Called to faith: one Lord, one faith, one baptism
I2. Called to action: life in the Spirit
I3. Called to receive: the God who communicates
I4. Called to belong: baptism and confirmation
I5. Called to serve: baptism and confirmation
I6. Called to worship: Holy Communion

Stage 4 Proclaiming Jesus
4.1 Through the Holy Spirit
4.2 In Our Lives
4.3 As His Witnesses
4.4 In The World
4.5 Day by Day

Brushing up on Believing[9]
1. God the Father
2. God the Son
3. God the Holy Spirit
4. Sons and daughters of God
5. Being Christ in the world
6. The Last Things

Part Two of the book has six sessions on the Lord's Prayer.

My Confirmation Notebook[10]
1. The reality of God
2. God in the modern world
3. Why confirmation?
4. Jesus of Nazareth
5. The meaning of Jesus
6. The Bible
7. Sin and forgiveness
8. The death of Jesus
9. The resurrection
10. The Holy Spirit
11. Prayer (1)
12. Prayer (2)
13. The sacraments

	14. The meaning of Holy Communion 15. Holy Communion Rite A 16. Holiness 17. Heaven and hell 18. Other religions 19. "One to Twelve" 20. The Church 21. The Church of England 22. Giving and receiving 23. Some basic Christian texts
Your Confirmation[11] ***Christian Beginnings*** 1. How to become a Christian 2. How to be sure you are a Christian 3. How to grow as a Christian ***Christian Belief*** 4. Belief in God the Father 5. Belief in Jesus Christ 6. Belief in the Holy Spirit ***Christian Behaviour*** 7. Moral standards 8. Bible reading and prayer 9. Fellowship and Holy Communion 10. The service of Christ	**Saints Alive**[12] 1. What is a Christian? 2. The person and work of Christ 3. The significance of the resurrection 4. Pentecost: then and now 5. The fruits and gifts of the Spirit: preparation to receive ministry — teaching on repentance and faith 6. Knowing Christ in the power of the Spirit — an opportunity for personal response 7. Christian growth 8. Membership of the Church 9. A shared meal and eucharist

Some principles to follow

As you will see, the published courses and books differ from each other a great deal while preserving certain common themes. The differences are partly because each is written for a slightly different purpose, and partly due to different emphases in theology and understanding of the Christian life.

Are there any general principles which can be drawn out about devising a syllabus for an evangelism nurture group? There seem to me to be six:

1. The course needs to cover the basics of Christian belief about the Father, Jesus, and the Holy Spirit. This needs to be covered in a systematic way and at the beginning of the course meetings.
2. Because the course will contain those who are enquirers and also those who are very new Christians there needs to be a simple and full statement of the Christian Gospel. The need to respond to the Gospel needs to be made very clear to the group. Space needs to be given in the syllabus and group meetings for this.
3. New Christians need to learn how to grow. Therefore, there needs to be teaching on principles of Christian growth and on such things as prayer, Bible reading and fellowship.
4. The course aims to lay a foundation for Christian living. This means there is a need to cover such areas as ministry, lifestyle, etc. which are not part of doctrine or of growing as a Christian.
5. People's questions should be given space, listened to and answered where possible. This means that the questions we all ask – on suffering, on other faiths, on science and religion – need to be covered during the course. It does not necessarily mean that these questions need a whole session to themselves. For all kinds of reasons it is best to focus on the positive.
6. There needs to be space in the first and last sessions to make a good beginning and a good ending. The content of these two sessions in particular should not be too rich.

In the light of the suggestions from the published material, go back now to your own syllabus. Are you satisfied with it? Are there any changes you need to make? In particular does it satisfy these three criteria:

Does it match your own beliefs? Can you teach and recommend the course with integrity?

Does it reflect the beliefs and priorities of the church in which it will be used?

Does it meet the needs of those who will be members of the evangelism nurture group?

Christians for Life

The syllabus for our Christians for Life course is offered here for reflection. Five years of teaching and developing the course have convinced me that the syllabus works: that it contains all the elements which are important for an evangelism nurture group, and that they are tackled in a sensible order. The course has undergone three major revisions in the five year period, and each time the order and titles of some of the sessions has changed. No doubt the course has not yet reached its final form.

The course falls into three parts. Part one (six sessions) covers what Christians believe from the very first question of God's existence to the session on becoming a Christian. Part two (four sessions) is about how Christians grow based on Luke's priorities in Acts 2:42. Part three consists of five sessions on Christian living.

PART ONE: WHAT CHRISTIANS BELIEVE

1. **God is there and he matters**
   The evidence for God's existence – in the universe and in ourselves. The natural place to begin for enquirers and for new Christians.

2. **We need God in our lives**
   The parable of the two sons and our journey away from God. Our need of God developed by looking at the space in our hearts, the walls that we build, and our fear of the future. We find this to be a key session. Significantly, none of the published courses outlined above focus on this need of God.

3. **Jesus – his ministry and death**
   A Bible-based session giving a survey of Luke's gospel. The first part looks at the question: "Who is Jesus?". The second half of the session is a presentation of the story of the passion.

4. **The resurrection of Jesus**
   The meaning of the cross is explored, following on from session three. The session goes on to look at the resurrection

accounts, the evidence for the resurrection, and what the resurrection of Jesus means for us today.

5. **The Holy Spirit**
    The promise of the Holy Spirit in the Old Testament and in Jesus' ministry. The day of Pentecost. The Holy Spirit's work in our lives: he dwells within us; he makes us more like Jesus; he gives us gifts for ministry. Questions almost always focus on the gifts of the Holy Spirit and receiving the Holy Spirit.

6. **Becoming a Christian**
    A summary of the Christian Gospel and of our response. For those who have become Christians already this is a useful summary of all they have learned so far, and an opportunity to reflect on their journey. For those who are not yet Christians the session is a chance to explain very simply what the Gospel is and how we respond. Praying with individuals in response to this session is explored in chapter ten.

In many ways, the basic viewpoint of the course until this point is evangelistic. Each session contains the Gospel and a gentle challenge to respond. The group have been addressed "as if" they were a group of interested enquirers. For part two the viewpoint changes. Now the group is addressed "as if" they are all new Christians. In fact there will probably be new Christians, enquirers and established Christians at each stage of the group's life.

PART TWO: HOW CHRISTIANS GROW

7. **Learning to pray**
    The transition to part two is marked by a Bible study on the parable of the sower, and a discussion of Christian growth and the need to persevere. The session then covers the importance of prayer; personal prayer and praying with others. Different ways of praying are explored in the worship time during the remainder of the course. I have found,

through experience, it is more helpful to deal with personal prayer before coming on to Bible reading than to deal with the Bible first.

8. **Reading the Bible**
Why is the Bible special? The background to the Old and New Testaments. The Bible as a library. Different ways of reading the Bible. An introduction to Bible reading notes.

9. **Belonging to the Church**
The importance of belonging to the church. New Testament pictures of the Church. Four ways of belonging: to the universal Church; the denomination; the congregation; the small group. Joining the church through baptism and confirmation. The story of our own church. The vision and priorities of our own church. These last two elements are very important. People need to know the history of a congregation to find their own place within it and to gain a sense of belonging. It's important also for the vision and direction of a church to be communicated to new Christians. If time allows, questions in this session have focused on the differences between denominations.

10. **Holy Communion**
This session combines simple teaching about the Holy Communion with a shared, informal Holy Communion service. The session gives a chance to focus on worship and prayer, and for the members of the group to lead parts of the service and share testimonies. It's made clear that everyone is welcome to receive Communion at this special service, whether or not they have been confirmed.

The course changes again at this point. The style and subjects in part two mean that there is a lot of input "from the front", although this is combined with exercises and questions. F om session eleven onwards, as well as exploring different issues in Christian living, members of the group are preparing for the course to come to an end. Everyone is encouraged to become part of a home group once Christians for Life finishes. The style of the meetings becomes much more like that of a home group, over the last five sessions, with more group Bible study; more emphasis on worship and prayer times; more exercises and less input from the course leader.

PART THREE: LIVING THE CHRISTIAN LIFE

11. Living God's way

God's standards for human living in the Ten Commandments and the rest of Scripture. The importance of lifestyle reflecting belief. Fighting the battle against sin, the world and the devil (picking up the words in the baptism service). A clear warning is given in this session about past and present involvement in occult activity. This may lead on to personal ministry outside of the group session (see chapter eleven). The session ends with a discussion of wider ethical issues and a summary of the strength God gives us for the battle.

12. Serving the Lord

The session covers ministry and service to God, inside and outside the church. We are all part of God's team. Different Christians are given different gifts. The group know each other well by this time and there is space in this session for several affirmation exercises, where people's gift and qualities are identified by others. The idea of calling to a ministry is explored as well, together with a number of pitfalls.

13. Your money and your life

The Christian attitude to money, to work and to giving. Biblical material is explored and there is a practical session, led by the PCC treasurer, on the church budget and where the money goes. The session gives an opportunity to explore how the church is managed. We have found it important over the years to explain the responsibilities of giving clearly to new Christians, whilst not putting them under any pressure to take action immediately.

14. **Learning to love**

A session on love, as the highest aim of the Christian life; on the way our relationships change as we grow as Christians. The session gives an opportunity for self-examination and for exploring the importance of forgiveness. The idea of God healing our emotions and characters by the work of his Holy Spirit is explored. Again, this often leads on to different opportunities for individual ministry outside the group meetings.

15. **Sharing the faith**

The session stresses the importance of faith-sharing; gives a chance to summarize the main points of the Gospel again, and for people to share their stories with each other at the end of the course.

By session twelve or thirteen people will know whether they are going to join a home group and should have made contact with their new group leader.

By the end of Christians for Life, group members have received a thorough grounding in the basics of Christian belief; each one knows how to keep growing and learning in the Christian life; many of the important issues which will recur now and in the future have been dealt with in a thorough way. Once again, it would be foolish to suggest that all the group members have reached the same point in their journey by the end of the course: much depends on where they were at the beginning. All will have moved on a long way and be ready for the next stage of the journey.

Material for the course

Once you have agreed your ideal syllabus it is the time to decide what teaching material to use. The temptation is to do the operation the other way round: to go down to the local Christian bookshop and buy the off-the-peg course which has the glossiest cover and the best reviews. It's much better to do the initial planning first, so you know what you are looking for.

In terms of format, there are basically three components to material for evangelism nurture groups. These are:

Material for the course leader, providing an outline for the sessions, sample talks and headings, discussion exercises, etc.

Material for course members, in the form of hand-outs, booklets to read, Bible readings, and other material for preparation.

Presentation material for the sessions such as videos, audio cassettes and visual aids.

A good example is *Saints Alive*, which has the three components of a leader's handbook, a course members' manual, and a video to use in several of the sessions.

Some courses are simply in book form (like *Your Confirmation*). These depend on your group members being able and prepared to read a chapter each week. Some provide a booklet for course members; others loose-leaf sheets.

Once the initial work of planning a syllabus has been done you will have three practical choices about materials: you can adopt, adapt or create your own from scratch.

Adopting is the least work and the least trouble, and works very well in many situations. Simply buy the course which best suits your own situation in terms of syllabus, theology and presentation. Get to know it well and put it into practice. Follow the guidelines for leaders' training. Don't be afraid to add ideas of your own or to change things that don't work. Many groups have run very well following this approach, providing the leaders have prayed and prepared well.

Adapting is more work but can bring greater rewards, in that a course can be tailored to fit your own requirements. If your evangelism nurture course is going to be a keystone of the church's growth in the years to come, it is well worth taking the time and trouble to produce a course which is right for the situation and the church at the time.

There are different ways of adapting. The first is simply to use one published course as your base and change it around to suit your own needs. Two or more courses can be combined. Or you can write your own syllabus and then employ the best material from each of the published courses.

Even if you decide to use just one published course as a base for group meetings, it is good to obtain several for reading and preparation before the sessions. A list of useful books is given in the resources section.

Adapting means you may need to adapt or produce your own course hand-outs. It's enormously helpful to course leaders and group members to have simple, photo-copied reminders of the main points from each session. The hand-outs build up into a useful file, which group members can keep and look back on in the years to come. We supply each member of a Christians for Life group with a simple, plastic wallet and cover sheet at the first meeting. Many have kept their notes over the years and often return to them.

A simple, typed or hand-written sheet which is photo-copies is adequate as a base. Content is more important than appearance. The appearance of the sheet can be improved by using different typefaces, enlarging the text on a photo-copier, pasting on illustrations or, if you have access to one, using a Desk Top Publishing computer.

Course hand-outs will be used again and again and so are well worth investing time and money in preparation. They give the course a fixed form, which means it can be used more easily by different leaders: the central core of the teaching is written down. It also means there is a common body of central teaching to which the whole church can refer as a basis for growth.

Creating is the third option. Don't be afraid to have a go. A lot of work is needed to develop a course to the standards of material now being published. But the more fresh ideas and insight brought into this whole area of Chrsitian ministry the better. Often your own material, as it develops over the years, will have a much more practical testing than some of the published courses.

But you need to be able to put a great deal of energy and time into preparing the material, especially first time around.

Part two of *Growing New Christians* has answered the preliminary questions about evangelism nurture groups. The role of the group has been related to church size, to the culture of the community, and the public worship of the congregation. The syllabus has been planned and the material chosen. Part three goes on to look at the practical side of leading the group.

Notes to chapter 6

1. *Caring for New Christians* (London: Bible Society and Scripture Union, 1982).
2. Discovery Groups are outlined in Michael Green's *Evangelism through the local Church* (London: Hodder and Stoughton, 1990) pp. 438 ff.
3. David Watson, *Discipleship* (London: Hodder and Stoughton, 1981).
4. Gavin Reid, *To be Confirmed* (London: Hodder and Stoughton, 1977).
5. Andrew Knowles, *Finding Faith* (Tring: Lion, 1983).
6. John Wimber, *The Dynamics of Spiritual Growth* (London: Hodder and Stoughton, 1990). Although the book is not designed to be a course on Christian basics, it is based on this material.
7. *Christian Basics*, P. Simmonds (Ed) (Warwick: CPAS, 1991). For a full description of the kit see the resources section. The sections given here are not designed to be used consecutively.
8. Stephen Cottrell and Martin Warner (eds), *Follow Me* (Birmingham: Additional Curates Society, 1991).
9. Gavin Reid and Sheilagh Brown, *Brushing Up on Believing* (London: Bible Reading Fellowship, 1990).
10. Hugh Montefiore, *My Confirmation Notebook* (London: SPCK, 1984).
11. John Stott, *Your Confirmation* (London: Hodder and Stoughton, 1991), with a study guide by Lance Pierson.
12. John Finney and Felicity Lawson, *Saints Alive* (Derby: Anglican Renewal Ministries, 1990).

PART THREE

Leading a Group

7
Leaders and advance planning

Planning an evangelism nurture group needs to begin several months before the group is due to start. The group needs to secure a place in the church's diary and in the minister's schedule. In our own church Thursday evenings has become established as Christians for Life night. Nothing else happens on that evening which would conflict with Christians for Life. Time is needed to draw materials together (if this is the first group of its kind) and to draw the group together.

Planning several months in advance almost always means that our planning needs to be by faith rather than by sight. It's not possible to know at that distance who will be part of a new group. Often potential group members will only make the decision to come in the last week or two before the starting date. We have found time and again that undertaking evangelism and nurture in this way is very like fishing, as Jesus suggested it would be. Every time we let down the nets by offering a group, God causes them to be filled.

Clergy and lay-led groups

Clergy-led groups

Once the syllabus has been decide the church needs to agree who should actually lead the groups.

In many situations it is important that the leader of the church should also lead the evangelism nurture group. There are several advantages to this, in terms of the overall growth of the church, as outlined in chapter four.

- By spending time with new Christians and enquirers the church leader is able to get to know them (and they him).
- The leader is able to have first-hand experience of the questions and problems of new Christians and church members in this particular area and church. This can feed back into the preaching, and pastoral and evangelistic ministry of the church.
- He or she is also able to be in close pastoral contact with group members at the beginning of their Christian life. Once the foundation of a relationship is laid through an evangelism nurture group it is easy to maintain and build that relationship with the future.
- Leading an evangelism nurture group is an excellent way to identify people's gifts and suggest ideas for future ministry.
- The church leader is able to monitor the helpfulness of the worship, preaching and other events in the life of the church from the point of view of new Christians.

There are many calls on the time of any person in ministry and especially on a person leading a church which is growing. Nevertheless, I would argue that playing a prominent role in the evangelism nurture structure is an important part of any minister's calling. In terms of time, the commitment is one evening each week most weeks of the year, together with time for planning and preparation.

Looking back now, over more than four years of leading Christians for Life groups in St George's, it is hard to see any area of ministry where my own time has been better spent. By God's grace there are many people who have become established in those groups and have gone on to exercise a significant ministry in the church and community. But I know that I myself have benefited enormously from the privilege of leading them. The benefits have come through friendship given and received; through learning from the questions and the insights of each group; through doing theology again and again with new Christians; and most of all through the privilege of seeing God at work through human lives. Many is the week when I have reached Thursday evening tired, a bit battered, dried out and knowing I have little to offer in myself. By the end of the evening, simply through being with a group of people keen to learn about their faith, I have found myself encouraged, refreshed and amazed at the grace of God. For me, any leader who does not take up the opportunity of leading groups for evangelism and nurture is missing out on one of the greatest opportunities and privileges of ministry.

We need to remember that Jesus' priorities and Paul's are with those who are on their way into faith. In the parable of the lost sheep the ninety-nine are left in the sheep-fold. It is the shepherd's job to spend his time seeking the lost. Paul writes that in terms of Christian nurture he is the skilled master builder (*sophos architekton* in the Greek). He is the one who lays the foundations and the first courses of bricks (1 Corinthians 3:10). These ensure that the building will stand secure, that the windows and the doors are in the correct places, and that the right angles are true. The remainder of the building is left to the apprentices in training under the master builder's supervision. There is a strong case in many churches for evangelism nurture groups to be led by the clergy.

If the minister or vicar is to lead, however, there is still a need for two or three lay co-leaders. The three or four then form a team for prayer, planning and sharing in the leading of the meetings, for the pastoral care of group members and for reflection.

Lay-led groups

Despite the arguments given above, there will be many situations where it is best that the groups are lay-led. The church leader may simply not have the gifts required to lead an evangelism nurture group. Or there may not be a full-time minister in the church at all. Or there may be a need for more than one group at a time, as in the programme church. In all of these situations, and doubtless others, it will be important to have lay-led groups.

It goes without saying (almost) that just because an ordained person leads the group it does not mean that the group will be better in any way from the group led by the lay team. It may even be worse, in terms of content, presentation and group dynamic. However, the important difference is that the group led by the church leader himself will be automatically tied in to the whole life of the church. With the lay-led group extra care needs to be taken to ensure this happens.

If the minister is not to lead the evangelism nurture group he needs to be involved at several stages along the way: in the planning and preparation; in reflection and review; in giving some of the teaching input; and in the on-going care of group members.

Often people argue that delegation is important because delegation saves time and means that the task can be done more effectively. This can be true in the long term. However, it is very important to realize that proper delegation, in the short term, takes as great an investment of time as doing the job yourself. It's a good rule of thumb never to delegate any task while you are under pressure yourself. If you do, the chances are the delegation will not happen smoothly and within a very short time the job will be back with the person it started with, or else will not be done well. Delegation requires time for preparation, training, supervision and reflection.

The qualities of group leaders

What kind of qualities are needed in those who lead evangelism nurture groups, whether the people are clergy or lay? If we are not careful we may end up having expectations like these, of others as well as ourselves.

Leading a group for evangelism and nurture is not always an easy task. Dorothy's story in chapter five showed how threatening a first meeting can be for a member of the group. But how does it feel from the other side?

We have recently had the experience within St George's of relaunching our home groups and appointing new leaders. After prayer and consultation with the congregation, eleven leaders were invited to lead new groups and to head up small teams of co-leaders. At the first meeting of the new leaders almost

WANTED

LEADERS FOR EVANGELISM NURTURE GROUP

Master's Degree in Theology required (Ph.D. preferred)

Full training in pastoral counselling expected

Qualification in Group Dynamics essential

Must be prepared to spend two hours each day in prayer for the group

Expert Biblical Knowledge

Able to answer the most obscure questions instantly

Only archangels and apostles need apply

everyone had been surprised, if not shocked, to be asked.
Everyone, without exception, felt (and still feels) inadequate to
the task.

Imagine another fictional – but not untypical – situation. Roger
is one of very few Christian men of his generation in his small
church. The vicar is about to leave but an evangelism nurture
group is needed during the interregnum. To his surprise, Roger
is invited to lead it. Let's listen to him as he prays, and to God's
replies, before, during and after the group meets . . .

Roger: Lord, Frank asked me to lead the new group tonight.
                I'm amazed he asked me. I felt sure after the PCC it
                would be George or Brenda. They've been Christians
                much longer than I have. I think they were a bit
                surprised as well – perhaps a bit jealous. I'm pleased
                to be asked but I'm going to have to say ''No''. I
                couldn't possibly do it, could I? I don't know all that
                the vicar knows. I couldn't answer their questions or
                lead the sessions. It's too much of a responsibility.
                I'll definitely say ''No'' on Sunday – is that all right?
                Amen.

The Lord: ''Do not say, 'I am only a child.' You must go to
                everyone I sent you to and say whatever I command
                you. Do not be afraid of them, for I am with you and
                will rescue you . . . I have put my words in your
                mouth.''
                Jeremiah 1:7–9

                              *   *   *

Roger: Lord, I did say ''Yes'' in the end. If you're calling me,
                I can't say ''No''. Just help me to do it right. Frank's
                promised me every support. Gladys and John are
                going to help. Thanks for that – I really get on with
                both of them. The material looks good. I've been
                reading it through tonight. We're going to visit all of

the group over the next three weeks. I expect they'll be put off once they've met me. Please help me. I've never done any visiting before. We start tonight. It's one of those first time things. Amen.

Later that night

Roger: Lord, it was great — it was like you'd been there before us. We really got on well with the people we met. They are looking forward to coming like anything. You've obviously been working already. Please bless them through the group and help us with the rest of the visits. Amen.

* * *

Roger: Lord, can't we just drop the whole idea now? How about a dose of flu? The group starts tonight. I just know I'm going to mess it up. For a start, hardly anyone's going to come. They don't know each other and no one will speak at all. I'm very worried about how the talk will go. The whole thing is just going to be one big disaster. Lord, why did I ever get into this? Amen.

The Lord: ''Be strong and courageous. Do not be terrified; do not be discouraged, for the Lord your God will be with you wherever you go.''

                Joshua 1:9

Later than evening . . .

Roger: Lord, it was amazing. You should have been there. It was a bit of a shaky start when they were all arriving. One or two didn't make it. But that first exercise really worked. Once they started people just didn't want to stop talking. Even the talk wasn't too bad. I got a bit stuck with one or two questions at the end, but there weren't any disasters. John and Gladys chipped in at just the right moment. We're off to a great start.

* * *

A few weeks later

Roger: Lord, that was awful tonight. Half the group didn't come and several never sent their apologies. Those that did come arrived late. There were only five there at five past eight. None of the exercises worked and Henry dominated the entire meeting with questions and stories about mediums. And this was the session when we'd decided to give a challenge to real commitment . . . Even the coffee was cold. That's it, as far as I'm concerned. I told you I was going to fail and now I have. It's the last time you'll get me doing anything like this. I'll just stick to handing out the books from now on . . .

What do you mean you never said it would be easy? You really think there might have been a spiritual battle going on tonight? In our group? The discussion did have a funny feel to it towards the end — like we were constantly going off track. So where do we go from here?

The Lord: ''Love is patient, love is kind. It does not envy, it does not boast, it is not proud. . . . it is not self-seeking, it is not easily angered, it keeps no record of wrongs. Love does not delight in evil but rejoices with the truth. It always protects, always trusts, always hopes, always perseveres.''

''Be strong in the Lord and in his mighty power. Put on the full armour of God so that you can take your stand against the devil's schemes . . . Pray in the Spirit on all occasions with all kinds of prayers and requests . . . Be alert and always keep on praying for all the saints.''

1 Corinthians 13:4—7, Ephesians 6:10—11, 18

After the last meeting

Roger: Lord, thank you. Leading that group was one of the
              best things I've ever done. There were lots of mistakes
              along the way. I've learned a lot of lessons and I know
              I could do it better if I were asked again. But I feel
              so close to the people now — and they all seem so
              close to each other. The prayer times over the last
              few weeks have been so deep. I was almost in tears
              as people gave their testimonies tonight and shared
              how belonging to the group has helped them. Lord,
              I know better than they do that it's been nothing to
              do with me at all. It's been your doing and I've been
              privileged to be part of it. Thank you. Alleluia. Amen.

              P.S. Lord, if ever you want me to do it again . . .

The Lord is gracious and compassionate, slow to anger and of
steadfast goodness — even to leaders of evangelism nurture
groups, even when we get it wrong.

It's worth repeating: the whole work of evangelism and nurture
is the Holy Spirit's work, not ours. Again, Paul sums up the
mystery: "For I planted and Apollos watered, but God gives the
growth. For neither he who plants nor he who waters is anything,
but only God who gives the growth." 1 Corinthians 3:6–7

Whether you are ordained or lay, leading a group can be a
threatening experience. Even vicars get the shakes sometimes;
even the clergy fail and feel inadequate for the task — at least
this one does. Some of my failures have been very real.
Experience helps, so do knowledge and skills, but in the end the
essential qualification for leadership is being called to the task by
God. If God has called you to this ministry, he will equip you
for the task, supply all that is needed and will anoint what you do.

Be sure, as well, that God supplies every gift that is needed
to help his church to grow. If this is the right time to establish
groups for evangelism nurture in your church then the leaders
are there somewhere. It's a matter of planning by faith, not by
sight.

Leaders for evangelism nurture groups need to be open people: open to God and open to others. We need to be reasonably mature and confident in our faith. There needs to be an integrity to our lives. We need to have a desire to see God at work in bringing people to faith and to mature discipleship. If we have those qualities then they are the right ones for the task and God can use us. Go for it!

Skills for group leaders

Qualities are more important than skills for group leaders. But if the right qualities are there, we can be more effective in the ministry as we come to master the skills as well. These are some of the areas where you will find you need to grow as your ministry in leading these groups develops:

In praying for others   Intercession remains a core part of the work. The more we learn about prayer, the more effective we can be. Praying for others in the leader's own prayer time is effective – simply name the people before God from a list of the group. During the life of a group I make it my aim to pray for group members each day. I have never remotely succeeded in meeting that aim – but there has been a lot of prayer along the way. Praying with others is important too – for which see chapters ten and eleven.

In teaching and leading the group   There is a lot that can be learned about giving a good presentation; about leading discussions; about the way adults learn. Some of this is covered in chapter nine. Strive for clarity and simplicity in talks. Go for honesty in discussions. Encourage questions and debate.

In pastoral care   A lot of the work in the group will take place outside of group meetings: in one-to-one meetings, telephone calls, practical care that is shown. Pastoral care is not a technical subject. It's about loving people and listening to them. Sadly, most of us grow very slowly in these areas, but the more we grow here the more effective we are.

In spiritual discernment   In a fascinating passage in John 5 Jesus tells us that he can only do what he sees the Father doing (John 5:19). It is very important in any Christian ministry, but especially in an evangelism nurture group, constantly to be watching for what the Father is doing in individual lives and in the life of the group. Is a person coming close to a point of commitment? Is someone being challenged about their lifestyle? Is there a past hurt which has been exposed and needs God's healing love? Is this the right time to introduce open prayer? Is there something that needs to be said right at the end of a meeting?

The same spiritual discernment needs to be exercised in the spiritual battle fought in the lives of the leaders and of the group. Those engaging in this ministry are on the front line of the battle and need the prayer support of the whole church. Be on guard against every form of spiritual attack, from discouragement to practical things or relationships going wrong on the day of a meeting. Once you have discerned some kind of spiritual attack pray specifically against it, preferably with another Christian. Be on the watch for the enemy's activity within the life of the new Christian or enquirer as well. Chapter eleven gives some guidelines here.

Spiritual discernment is a gift rather than a skill; it is given rather than acquired. Ask God for eyes to see what is happening at this level within the life of the group. Have the faith and the courage to respond to what you see.

Preparing the leaders

The small team of leaders, however it is formed, needs to prepare together for leading the group. Depending on the experience of the group there may be a need for some training. The training could be based on relevant chapters of this book. The CPAS *Christian Basics* pack also contains an excellent training course for leaders.

Whether or not there is a training element to the leaders' meetings, there certainly needs to be practical preparation.

Practical preparation needs to include:

130   *Growing New Christians*

PREPARING THE LEADERS: CHECK-LIST AND AGENDA

1. *Prayer together*
   The picture of the group being like a windsurfer is a useful one. If the power of the Spirit is moving through the group, the leader's task is to guide and direct. If the wind isn't blowing, no amount of leadership can move people forward.

2. *Materials and syllabus*
   These need to be agreed, available and understood. Co-leaders should have plenty of time to prepare any session input. Videos should be watched in advance. Special equipment (like TV and video) should be obtained where necessary. The better the leaders know the material from beginning to end, the better the group will flow.

3. *Venue and practical details*
   Don't use the corner of the draughty church hall. Use a place where people can feel at home: someone's house or else a church lounge. When I was confirmed, aged eleven, the confirmation candidates all sat in the choir stalls of the church, with frozen arms and numb bums. Having said that, half of our last Christians for Life course was conducted in the middle of building-site conditions, as our church house was being refurbished. Attendance actually went up. Meeting in the same place throughout the group's life is important. As well as the venue, you will need to make practical arrangements and decisions about refreshments, transport, etc.

4. *The first session*
   This needs to be planned in some detail in advance (see below).

5. *Publicity*
   This needs to be attractive, well presented and available. Some suggestions are given below.

6. *Gathering the group together*
   You need to decide how this should happen. Will you write, call or phone? Who will make which approach? Hints and ideas are given below.

Publicity

A key element in publicity is a printed invitation to the group. This can be brief and attractive with a simple title. I have found it more effective to have a folded leaflet, giving a full description of what the group is about and who is invited to come. On the next page is a sample of the publicity for a Christians for Life group in St George's.

The leaflet can be left at the back of church; it can be distributed to all those involved in contact programmes; and copies can be given to church staff and leaders of organizations – all of whom can then encourage contacts to come along.

Publicity to the group should also be given in the church magazine and/or news-sheet. Publicity through announcements in church is also essential.

It can be helpful to make the first announcements and have publicity available about two months before the group is due to start meeting. A surprising number of people plan and think that far in advance. Announcements should then be more frequent just before the group begins. It is good to ask people to make a definite commitment to coming and to let the group leaders know if they plan to join. This means you will know how many to expect on the first night and roughly who will be there.

Whatever means you have for publicity in your church, make the best use of it for these groups. No matter how good or extensive

An invitation to:

Christians
for Life

You are warmly invited to join our new CHRISTIANS FOR LIFE GROUP which begins in June.

WHO IS THE GROUP FOR?

The group is for anyone who would like to learn more about the Christian faith.

You may like to join us if:

☐ you have recently started coming to church and would like to go deeper

☐ you have been a Christian for some years but you would value a refresher in the Christian faith.

☐ you have recently become a Christian and you would like to become established in the basics of the faith.

☐ you would like to be baptised or confirmed.

WHAT WILL HAPPEN?

The Christians for Life course aims to give basic teaching on what Christians believe, on how Christians grow and on practical Christian living today.

There will be some input each week followed by discussion and a chance to ask questions.

WHEN AND WHERE?

The group will be meeting on Thursday evenings, beginning on Thursday 4th June

The group will be led by Steve Croft with assistance from other members of the church.

We will meet for fifteen sessions in all.

All of the meetings will be at the Vicarage in Bracewell Drive at 8.00 p.m.

your written publicity, however, it alone will draw very few people along to a new group.

Gathering the group together

This has to be done, in the end, by prayer and personal invitation. A list of likely or possible people can be compiled by the church staff and by leaders of organizations. It is then important to spend time with those people and, if it seems appropriate, to invite them along to the group.

It is always better if the initial invitation comes from a person who is already in a good pastoral relationship with the prospective group member, rather than the group leader. If the response is positive, then the group leader can call and say "hello" before the sessions begin. A person is naturally much more likely to say "no" to an invitation from someone they have hardly met. Never pressurize anyone into taking part in a group. For some it will just not be the right time. Leave an open door for a second invitation at some point in the future.

Once again, particularly in small and medium-size churches, the clergy will have a special role in inviting people along to the groups and, if they are not leading themselves, building good bridges between the group leaders and group members. If continuous evangelism nurture groups are to work the clergy need to be willing to spend a large amount of time visiting and building contacts with people on the fringe of the church, and inviting them to take part in the groups.

Our next group is about four weeks away from starting. We have a list of five people already committed to coming. Three of the five have volunteered to take part after reading publicity. One was invited after a conversation at the church Christmas party. The fifth person was someone I visited about her baby's baptism. She has been coming to church for some time, so we talked about the possibility of her coming to the new group and what that would involve. Like many people, Carol was relieved to hear she wouldn't need to say anything, and pleased to hear there would be systematic input, a chance to get to know people and plenty of chance to ask questions. Over the next three weeks there are about fifteen or more people I would like to ask to take part in the group. Some of these will mean a visit; others will be invited over coffee after church; others will be invited over the phone, if I already know them well. In all probability one or two more will join from the congregation in response to further announcements in church.

Gathering the group together is a very human exercise, yet there is always that sense, as well, that God has been working long before we ever came on the scene. It's probably one of the most important parts of the exercise. If the group is lay-led (and the leader not known to the majority of group members) I would strongly recommend a home visit to every prospective member by the leader or co-leader.

As a final reminder, in the week before the group starts, every person receives a printed card giving the date and starting time once again.

Just to remind you

CHRISTIANS FOR LIFE

*begins on Thursday 26th September
at 8.00 pm in St George's House*

See you there!

8

The content of a meeting

Three examples

The church as a whole have decided on a strategy for evangelism and nurture. The material to be used has been agreed. The leaders have been appointed and have done their planning. The publicity has been well-received and twelve people have agreed to take part in the group. Picture these three scenarios for the fourth meeting in the life of the group. Each of the groups is using the same syllabus, the same materials, and has broadly the same aims.

In church A the group is led by the Revd Smiley. Chairs are arranged in a circle around the fireside in the church lounge. Handouts have been distributed before the meeting. There is a somewhat tense atmosphere, even though the group has been running for several weeks now. One or two hushed, polite conversations happen around the room. There is a general shuffling of papers and coughing. People hardly seem to be on first name terms.

At 8.00 p.m. prompt, Revd Smiley opens in prayer. He welcomes the group somewhat formally, picks up his notes and begins the teaching on tonight's subject: the death and resurrection of Jesus.

The talk is good in parts. Following the notes on the printed sheets, Revd Smiley spends some time talking about the meaning of Jesus' death on the cross. He explores several different theories of the atonement, and is graphic in his description of the way Jesus' death deals with the group's sin.

After half an hour on the cross, without pausing for breath, Revd Smiley changes the subject to the resurrection. The group hear all about the different resurrection accounts. The evidence for the resurrection is recounted in great detail (seven different points are made each with four subheadings), and Revd Smiley concludes with a forceful exposition of 1 Corinthians 15.

Revd Smiley has finished speaking by about 9.15. The group sit and listen politely. The keener ones have brought clipboards and take notes. There is a chance then for the group to ask questions about all that has been said. One man with a large Bible asks for clarification on the meaning of 1 Corinthians 15:8. Revd Smiley gives a thorough answer, by which time it's half past nine.

One of the co-leaders closes the meeting in prayer and the meeting reverts to polite conversation made over coffee. Everyone is gone by ten o'clock and is told to look forward to next week's session on the Holy Spirit.

Church B, across the valley, has a very different approach. The group is being led by the curate, David Trump. Only a couple of people have arrived by eight o'clock. People are relaxed and friendly, though, and keen to talk. David is deep in conversation about the fortunes of the local rugby team. After a while the subject changes to the state of the local schools and then to the Government's education policy. All this while people are drifting into the meeting and more or less joining in with what is being said.

Around 8.25 David calls the meeting to some sort of order.

"Right then — last week we had a very interesting discussion. Our subject for tonight is the death and resurrection of Jesus. What do you think about all that?"

"I don't like all this talk about people coming back from the dead. It's like ghosts, isn't it?" says one of the group.

"You shouldn't dismiss it like that, though," says another. "I went to see Doris Stokes once . . ."

The discussion rambles on, just like the conversation before the meeting started. After ten minutes on ghosts and mediums there is a jump to Jehovah's Witnesses, then to the cost of funerals, then to whether people should wear crosses if they're not Christians. David's role seems to be to sit back and let people get on with it. Once, when one of the group asks him what he thinks he says quite deliberately: "It doesn't matter what I think. It's what you think that matters — ordinary, working people."

Straight away the discussion turns, as it has done most weeks, to why the church does not appeal to ordinary people. After about an hour of this, at 9.20, David draws the discussion to a close: ''That's been an absolutely fascinating discussion. We didn't get very far with the sheet tonight but not to worry. You can read that for yourself at home. The things we've been talking about have been the important ones. Next week we'll go on to think about the Holy Spirit.''

The group adjourns to the local pub.

In group C, Susan Jameson is the leader. The group members have mostly arrived by eight o'clock and the room is buzzing with conversation. One or two crack jokes as they arrive. People seem genuinely concerned about each other — talking as good friends do. There's a general air of anticipation in the room.

Susan calls the meeting to order after about five minutes and opens with a brief prayer. The first part of the meeting is an exercise in small groups of three: ''Talk to each other for a few minutes about your understanding of Jesus' death. How much do you know about what happened? How much does it mean to you?'' There's a bit of silence and then four or five different conversations begin around the room.

Kath, the co-leader, draws the group back together after seven minutes and introduces the next part of the programme: an extract from the video *Jesus of Nazareth*. It's the part where Jesus is crucified. The group watch in silence. One or two are visibly moved. Susan follows the video by talking very simply about the meaning of the death of Jesus, referring to the notes on the hand-out sheet. It seems right to bring this part of the meeting to a conclusion with a time of silence, a brief prayer and a song.

It's into groups again for the next part: ''What evidence do you think there is that Jesus rose from the dead?'' The groups spend about ten minutes on this one and then John, the other co-leader, draws the groups' conclusions together and writes them up on a large piece of paper.

There is a summary of the evidence for the resurrection on the hand-out and John gives a short talk, taking the group through this and on to the meaning of the resurrection for today. There are buzz groups again, where people simply comment on what they have heard and are asked to think of any questions. The whole group together then has a question and answer session, which goes on well after half past nine. Susan closes in prayer, draws people's attention to the Bible readings to be done during the week, and gives a two-sentence preview of next week's session on the Holy Spirit.

Coffee is served and people chat informally in small groups. Kath is praying quietly with two members of the group in the corner of the room. Many of the remainder are still talking and asking questions about the session. It's around 10.20 when the last of the group leave – a number of them continue the discussion in the pub down the road.

Which group will work best? The way a meeting is structured is very important. You are aiming to provide a meeting where group members can learn, get to know each other, relax and ask questions. In church A and church B the group leaders fail in their task because of the way they lead the group.

Revd Smiley is too directive. His group, he thinks, will learn the way he learned at college: by listening to erudite lectures. But the group is given too much to digest at once. There is no attempt to help people get to know each other and establish relationships. Attention wanders after the first ten minutes of listening to the talk. There is no encouragement to ask questions, because the questions only invite more long talks.

David Trump has made the opposite error. He knows long talks are a mistake (David hated his lectures at college). He feels less sure in his faith himself and so is willing to talk about almost anything but the central truths of Christianity. He has been taught that education is about drawing truth out of people and he mistakenly believes that happens by allowing the group to talk about whatever it wants to discuss. The one or two strong characters (there are some in every group) inevitably come to dominate the meeting, to the frustration of the rest. Very little is learned because there is no input whatsoever.

Susan's approach is much better. She uses her team well. People are encouraged to think and to discuss. The time is broken down into shorter sections, and different ways of teaching and learning are used throughout. In the course of the evening

Susan's group get to know each other better; they come to know the story of the cross: it's meaning for them; and the evidence for the resurrection of Jesus. There is plenty of space for questions and room to respond to God as well.

There are nine different elements which can be used in leading a meeting. All of them are important in different ways. There won't be space to use each one every time. The nine elements can be thought of as a menu. Each session is built up from different elements on the menu into a whole. Ideas for putting the elements together are given at the end of this chapter.

Story and testimony

Simple testimony can be extremely powerful, especially in the context of a group of people who know each other well. An effective way to use testimony is to have a person tell the story of how they became a Christian each week for the first six weeks of the group's life. This helps in a number of ways:

- Testimony is a powerful witness to the members of the group who are not yet Christians and backs up and supports the teaching being given. Testimony also builds up and supports the faith of those who are already Christians.
- The most important way of helping the group grow together and get to know each other is by learning each other's stories. This can be done in depth through testimony.
- Sharing their own story can often be significant for the person doing the telling. Preparing to speak, and then telling their story, can help put the whole journey of faith into perspective.

The compilers of the training course *Person to Person* rightly stress the importance of Christians telling their story in evangelism. In the *Person to Person* model a story is broken down into a before, how and after pattern. It is right to stress that not everyone will have had a "before"; some may not have much of an idea "how" they became a Christian (or with the passage of time it may become much less important); but everyone has

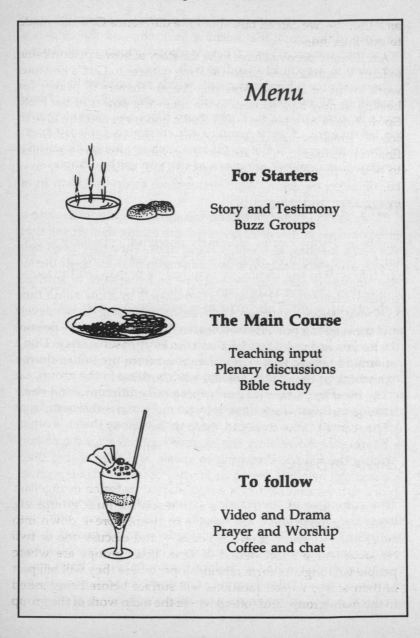

Menu

For Starters

Story and Testimony
Buzz Groups

The Main Course

Teaching input
Plenary discussions
Bible Study

To follow

Video and Drama
Prayer and Worship
Coffee and chat

an "after" – we can all talk about the difference God has made to our lives now.

A testimony does not have to be the story of how a person came to faith. A testimony is person bearing witness to God's gracious work in his or her life. This may be an answer to prayer for healing. It may be a witness to the renewing power of the Holy Spirit. It may be a testimony to God's goodness and the love of fellow Christians during a difficult time. It may be a story of God's financial provision or of answered prayer. Christians are called to bear witness to the mighty acts of God, whatever they may be, on every occasion. What better place to do that than in an evangelism nurture group?

There are four more points on testimony in groups. Be sure to give someone plenty of notice if you are asking them to tell their story in a meeting. A week is about right. They may need help in preparing what they will say. Be sure to pray for them during that time as it may well prove to be an experience of spiritual conflict and testing. I have learned always to allow some time to elapse between a person's conversion or healing (or whatever) and them giving public testimony to what has happened. Be sure the leaders and co-leaders tell their own story at some stage. Don't be afraid to bring guests into the group from the wider church to share their own faith. Finally, always stress to the group, on every occasion, that each person's story is different. God deals with us as individuals. Just because my story is different from yours doesn't mean one of us is a better Christian than the other.

Buzz groups

Story and testimony are good optional extras for an evangelism nurture group. Buzz groups are an essential. Buzz groups are when your group of eight, twelve or twenty break down into small units – twos, threes or fours – and discuss one or two questions for a short period of time. Buzz groups are where people will begin to form relationships; where they will tell part of their story; where questions will surface before being asked in the main group; and (often) where the main work of the group takes place. The groups can be used at the beginning of the meeting to break the ice and get people thinking; in the middle to help digest what has been said so far; and at the end to stimulate discussion and help group members form questions.

Here are some examples of different types of buzz group exercises and questions.

Some examples of different types of buzz group exercises and questions are given opposite.

prepare for the next part of the meeting, or to just quietly listen to what people are saying and get a sense of where the group is going. It's always good for co-leaders to join in with the buzz groups and add their wisdom to the discussion.

Buzz groups can only cope with one – or at the most two – questions at a time. Don't give them an agenda to work through! Think carefully about the questions you want the groups to tackle and stick to those. After some exercises it will be important for the buzz groups to share what they have said with the whole group. On other occasions that would be a waste of time. Be flexible.

Teaching input

In any course which aims to lay a foundation for Christian faith, growth and practice there does need to be a substantial teaching input. There may be exceptions, but generally speaking an adult who becomes a Christian in Britain today knows almost nothing about Christian faith or belief; almost nothing about the Bible; almost nothing about Church history (or, indeed, any kind of history at all).

The Church, as a whole, faces a massive challenge to teach. An evangelism nurture group can only lay a foundation: you can't cover everything and, even if you could, people would not be able to take it in. What is needed is concise, well-thought-out and clear input which is well-illustrated and well-delivered.

Most group leaders will depend on their course syllabus for the outline of their input and perhaps for content too. If you are using video material for some of your course, don't be a coward and rely on it for the whole of the teaching. However good the

BUZZ GROUP QUESTIONS AND EXERCISES

1. **Ice-Breakers**
   a. Ask each person to interview their partner and find out three facts about them and why they are here. Each person then introduces their partner to the group.
   b. Share in small groups the best and the worst thing that has happened to you this week.

2. **Sharing your Story**
   a. What are your best memories of living at home as a child?
   b. At what age did you leave home? Was it a good or a bad experience for you?
   c. What were your first impressions when you came to church? What was helpful? Was anything unhelpful?

3. **Small Group Exercises**
   a Share what you know about the subject for tonight. What are the main questions you have?
   b. Each small group discusses one imagined moral dilemma with conclusions presented to the whole group.

4. **Helping People to Digest**
   a. Just take a minute to talk to each other about what you've just heard. How did it strike you?
   Do you agree with what's been said?

5. **To Draw Out Questions**
   a. Break into small groups for a minute. There will be a lot of questions arising out of tonight's session. Which are the most important for you?

programmes are it would make the course very dull and impersonal. Remember to break the teaching down into smaller sessions, punctuating these with practical exercises, plenaries and buzz groups. Two, fifteen-minute talks in an evening are usually better than one of thirty minutes.

Although you may be basing what you say on a course outline or handbook, it's important to take the time to make the material your own. Read one or two other chapters of books besides your main course notes. Suggestions are given in part four. Think through what you want to say and get it clear in your own mind.

It often helps to write out a talk in full, even when it's to be given to a small group. After you have written it out and read it through a couple of times it shouldn't be necessary to refer to anything more than headings during the meeting itself. The talk can then be saved and used as a basis for the next course.

It's important, when you are giving a talk in a small group, to be as inter-active as possible. Give people permission to interrupt (although not too often). Talk to the group and maintain good eye contact: don't direct what you are saying to the floor or the ceiling. If you are building an argument check along the way that people understand each point: "Do you see what I mean?"; "Have you got that?"; "Still with me over there?"

It helps people to follow the talk if the main points are written on the course hand-out. Make sure the structure of what you are going to say is clear and logical. Use lots of illustrations and anecdotes: these will stay in the mind long after the main arguments have faded away. If you can, use visual aids – prepared beforehand or drawn on the spot. Artistic quality doesn't matter. Clarity does. Be confident in your material and in your delivery – and (at the risk of labouring the obvious) make sure you are audible.

Preparing a short talk can take a long time, even when you are using material prepared by others. Apart from the overall structure of the meeting, this is the aspect of preparation which will take longest. It can seem a hard slog. Don't despair. Through the work you are putting in God is able to build strong foundations in the lives of his people.

A STEP-BY-STEP GUIDE TO PREPARING A GOOD GROUP TALK

---

1. **Write down the aim.** Just one − the word "and" is not allowed in an aim for a talk.

---

2. **Get the structure clear.** What are the main points you are trying to get across? If you have more than four you will probably begin to lose the group's attention and your own way.

---

3. **Build in the illustrations.** The more, the better (within reason). Illustrations can be analogies, anecdotes; visual or anecdotal.

---

4. **Work hard on the beginning and the ending.** The beginning should be ear-catching, attractive and tell people where you are going. The ending should sum up where you've been and, if you can, end with a challenge.

---

5. **Write out the talk in full.** Reduce it to simple headings for the purpose of delivery.

---

6. **Make your delivery clear and confident.** Stick to the point and stick to time. Get good feedback during and after the talk and don't be surprised at what God is able to do.

Plenary discussions

Having time together as a whole group is another essential for each meeting. Although the time together does not always need to be in the same place in the meeting, towards the end is a natural place for a plenary session. A whole group discussion gives a chance to bind the group together and a chance for people to listen to each other, as well as to the group leaders.

There are four different ways of running a plenary session.

Feedback from the buzz groups   A "What did you think about subject x" buzz session can be fed back into the whole group. Depending on the subject, it's a good idea to write down answers and conclusions on a large piece of paper or overhead projector. You need to have the confidence as leader to go round each group systematically and ask for feedback. It's your responsibility to decide which questions can be tackled then and there, and which should be left until later. As each group offers their response remember to say thank you and affirm what is being said. People will gradually get over their unwillingness to speak aloud in a large group if they see that comments and questions are welcomed, not criticized.

Response to a piece of teaching/video   This will probably not work well in the early stages of the group's life, but will become a possibility as the group relax with each other.

Whole group exercises   Once people have come to trust each other it becomes possible to do an exercise with the whole group. One we have developed in Christians for Life, for the later stages, is to ask the group to imagine that our church is to plant a new congregation in a neighbouring area. The group is the pilot team. They have a grant of £500 and no premises. Their task is to decide the priorities and plan for the new church plant, and to decide which member of the group will take on which ministry. The group leader leaves the room for the exercise and returns to listen to the results. If the group can take on a common task (something simple, like organizing refreshments for a church event) that can have the same effect. People are planning together and setting goals as a group.

Question and answer sessions   These are probably the most important kind of plenaries. Every member of an evangelism nurture group will come with questions, even those who have been Christians for many years. Many more questions will be stimulated by the sessions each week. It's very important, for every group member, that these questions are asked, listened to, and answered to their satisfaction so that they are free to move on to the next stage of the journey.

Asking questions – and expressing doubts – needs to be encouraged in every way throughout the life of the group. Make sure the group is open to every kind of enquiry. People do not suspend their minds when they become Christians. Often they start to think more keenly than before. If we are asking a person to base their whole life here and for eternity on the claims of Jesus Christ, if we are asking them to make radical changes in life and lifestyle, it is only natural that people should test those claims (and those who make them) to the utmost limit.

In the first few sessions of the group, particularly, make it clear that question time is absolutely open for people to ask anything they want to ask – whether it's relevant to that theme or not. When you are answering questions here are some pointers:

- Always be honest and open. If you don't know the answer, say so. Make a commitment to do some homework in time to give an answer next week.
- Don't feel you have to defend God in the face of honest enquiry. He can stick up for himself.
- Give the answers which make sense to you – which you can believe in with an honest heart and mind. Don't feel tied too narrowly to defending party lines or doctrines, or things you think the vicar (or congregation) will approve of.
- Bear in mind that some questions don't have answers. It's helpful to make a distinction between a problem and a mystery. Problems are questions which have solutions ("Why does Mark's gospel have three different endings?"). Mysteries are things which cannot be explained: the more you look, the deeper they become. The Trinity is a mystery. Sometimes by talking and thinking you can understand the Trinity more clearly. But it remains a mystery. The Incarnation is a mystery too. So is the Atonement and the question of suffering.

- Beware of creeping fundamentalism which says: "The Bible says this so it must be right." Generally speaking, that answer will not satisfy a new Christian or an enquirer for whom the Bible has, as yet, no authority. Other arguments are often needed to supplement quoting chapter and verse.

The following table gives some of the more common questions which are likely to be raised at some point during an evangelism nurture group. A good training exercise for any group leader would be to work out your own answers to these questions in advance of the course starting.

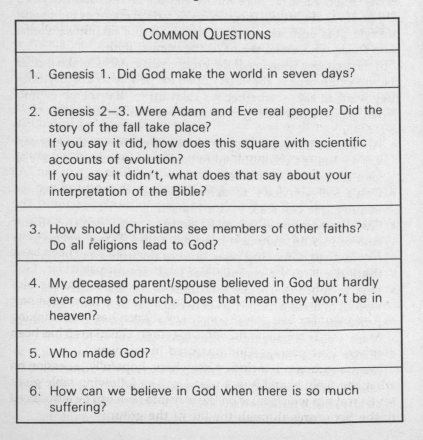

COMMON QUESTIONS
1. Genesis 1. Did God make the world in seven days?
2. Genesis 2–3. Were Adam and Eve real people? Did the story of the fall take place? If you say it did, how does this square with scientific accounts of evolution? If you say it didn't, what does that say about your interpretation of the Bible?
3. How should Christians see members of other faiths? Do all religions lead to God?
4. My deceased parent/spouse believed in God but hardly ever came to church. Does that mean they won't be in heaven?
5. Who made God?
6. How can we believe in God when there is so much suffering?

Bible study

Most groups of enquirers and new Christians do not cope well with the traditional form of Bible study where a group read a passage and work through a series of questions designed to draw out the meaning of the verses and to be springboards into discussion.

This method of studying the Bible is important in established home groups. However, enquirers and new Christians begin with a very sketchy knowledge of the Scriptures. Comprehension and reading skills may not be very developed. To be left alone in a small group with a passage to look at and a list of questions to answer can be an unhelpful experience for many.

However, to expose people to the Bible is very important and a key part of the group. The best way for this to happen is gradually and gently. In the early meetings verses which form a Bible base for the sessions can be printed on the hand-outs. Individual gospels can be used, rather than full Bibles. It's better to give people just one or two questions to think about in small groups rather than take the whole group through a printed list.

Try and use as many different and imaginative ways as you can of taking people into the Bible. During the life of the group try and introduce people to as much of the Bible as you can. As in many aspects of the group's life, your own attitude to the Scriptures will be "caught" by the group as much as taught. The Word of God has a power all of its own. Teaching and input is immeasurably stronger when there is a firm biblical base. Many of the most effective teaching sessions I have led have been basic expositions of well-known biblical passages. In particular, God uses the Scriptures to convict a person of sin, to use the old-fashioned language. For several of the men who have been part of Christians for Life groups a very key session has been thinking through the Ten Commandments together. Galatians 5 has been another short passage God has used in this way.

Every syllabus will include somewhere, hopefully, a session on what the Bible is and how to read it. The following table gives seven ways in which those on the way into faith can be introduced to the Scriptures through the life of the group:

SEVEN WAYS OF USING THE BIBLE

1. **Exegesis** of key texts by the course leaders. I would always include the prodigal son in one of the early sessions, the parable of the sower on Christian growth, the Ten Commandments on Christian living, and 1 Corinthians 13 on growing in relationships.

2. **Small group Bible study** There are many ways this can be done. Here are three:

   a. **"Search Exercises"** Ask the small group to look up a number of different passages on the same theme and discover what the Bible says about them.
   For example:
   Look up these verses in small groups and write down what each one is saying about the Bible, and why this book is special:
   2 Timothy 3:16
   Psalm 1:1−3
   Psalm 119:105
   Ephesians 6:17

   b. **Study of a particular Bible passage** in the traditional way, with one or two carefully framed questions.

   c. **Study of different passages** Each small group studies a different passage on the same topic. The groups then teach each other what they have learned.
   For example:
   Divide into small groups. Each group should take one of the passages listed below. Imagine that you are preparing a sermon for next Sunday on money and giving. Draw out the main teaching on money in your passage and then present your "outline sermon" to the whole group.
   1 Timothy 6:3−10
   Luke 12:13−21
   Luke 18:18−30
   Matthew 6:19−24
   2 Corinthians 9:6−7

3. **Use passages to support your argument in talks and input.** These passages can be printed on a hand-out sheet or read out at the time. It is important that people can see that all which is being taught is based upon the Bible.

   For example, refer to 1 Corinthians 12 when exploring spiritual gifts; to 1 Corinthians 15 when teaching on the resurrection, etc.

4. **Use the Bible to support your answers in question and answer sessions.** It's far better to base our answers on Scripture than just to pluck them out of our heads.

5. **Use the Bible in times of worship as a group.** Read from the psalms or the gospels regularly in worship times. Led meditations on particular passages can be very helpful indeed in showing people how to listen to God through the Scriptures.

6. **Encourage group members to study the Bible in preparation for the sessions.** It's an excellent thing for people to read through one of the gospels during the first part of the group's life. Some time may need to be given to help people through the next week's readings each session. Difficult questions can be answered week by week as well.

7. **Encourage people to develop a discipline of daily Bible reading.** This will mean introducing the group to Bible reading notes and aids at the right time, encouraging personal use of the Bible, and giving some time in the group meetings to discussing how things are going and to exploring difficulties.

The right way of using the Bible will obviously differ from group to group and situation to situation. In most cases it will be best that the Bible is "phased in", as the life of the group develops. One of the biggest fears in most people who come to an evangelism nurture group is that they will be made to look and feel ignorant. Take great care not to allow this to happen. Never ask people to read aloud unless they have prepared beforehand, or unless you know them well. Never put people on the spot. Take care that you have accurate expectations of the level of group members' knowledge.

Using video

There are various video teaching aids on the market which can be excellent, provided they are employed in the right way.

Match the video carefully to your group. Some are quite demanding to watch and, while they may help some groups, they will only confuse others. In every series of videos some are better than others. Don't be afraid to be selective. Watching television can kill discussion so try not to do too much of it in the meetings. It's good to follow the video slot with buzz groups to wake people up again and to get them talking.

Prayer and worship

How you develop the prayer and worship life of the group depends on where you are starting from and where you want to go. Learning to pray and worship with a small group is a very important part of the group's life. In our own context, in most groups we begin with a situation where we have no singing and just an introductory and concluding prayer said by the leader. We aim to reach the point where the group is able to pray and worship together, and is ready to become a home group (or else divide between several groups).

The progression looks something like this:

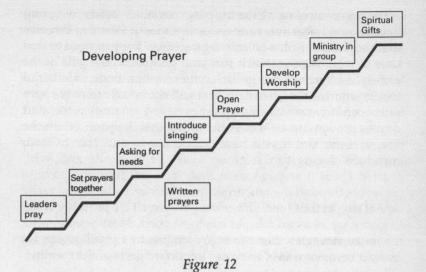

Figure 12

Significant points in the group's growth could include:

Leaders opening in prayer The more people can share in this the better. Prayers should be short, natural and to the point – the kind of prayers anyone can pray.

Saying prayers together Saying the Lord's Prayer together, or the grace is a simple, natural way of everyone praying aloud. It is possible to use other prayers or psalms in this way, if you are able to print out or project the words.

Asking for needs for prayer Extend the prayer time at the end of the meeting slightly by asking if anyone can suggest needs for prayer. The leader then leads the group in prayer for each one of these needs.

Group members writing prayers down A member of the group could be given a few days' notice (and offered help with preparation) and asked to lead prayers which he or she has written down, either at the beginning or at the end of the meeting.

Introducing singing Worshipping together binds a group together and helps everyone to focus on God. Worship can also be an important means of learning together. But you need to find ways of worshipping which suit your group and the gifts of the leaders. As long as your group contains a significant number of people who are not Christians you will not be able to move very far in worship. Lots of singing (or even any singing) at the start of most groups can be more off-putting than helpful. When the time is right, and if you have people ready and able to lead, introduce singing to the group's life. Be as gentle and light-hearted about it as you can at first. You will find you have to persevere through the embarrassment barrier. If the group really cannot sing in tune (and I have known several) it's probably better to give it up as a bad job. At least you tried. Most people, after the initial struggles, come to enjoy singing in a small group; for many it becomes one of the most important parts of the meeting.

Introducing open prayer This needs to be done prayerfully and carefully. You need to give a good explanation about why it is good for Christians to pray together. Allow people to talk honestly and openly about their fears and the barriers they have about praying aloud. Make it clear that no one should feel they have to pray aloud at any one time. Set an example in your own prayers by being short and to the point. When you are leading in prayer be sensitive to the silences: are they helpful or embarrassing? If a group is able to come through the "prayer barrier" together you will find that praying together adds something very important to the meetings.

Developing the worship There is a difference between singing choruses and worshipping God. Worship happens the more we "forget about ourselves and concentrate on him" as the song puts it. You may not have a gifted musician or worship leader in the leadership team for the group, so there may be a natural limit to the way worship can develop. But there may be others in the church who would come to the group for one or more sessions to give some teaching on worship and to take people further.

Praying for group members At certain times it may be right to pray for people in the group during a prayer time. This could be done at their request, or at the leaders' suggestion, and with the permission of the person concerned. Prayer may be for healing, for renewal, for any pressing personal or family need. Simply ask those sitting on either side of the person to lay their hands on their shoulder or head as a way of focusing the prayer of the whole group and then the leaders should pray aloud as seems right.

Using spiritual gifts From time to time the worship and prayer life of a group will grow to the point where it is possible to develop the use of spiritual gifts in worship and prayer times: particularly gifts of tongues, prophecy, word of knowledge and healing. Here, as in many other areas, the way in which the group is able to develop will depend on the experience and knowledge of the group leaders.

Alongside developing the worship in the group there is the task of helping those who have become Christians develop their own life of prayer. This can be done through a combination of teaching, discussion and feedback on what is happening; introducing new ideas and suggestions from time to time.

Coffee and chat

There isn't too much to say about this, except that it's important. The end is better than the beginning. It's here that friendships are cemented. The leader and co-leaders need to make good use of the time to talk individually with group members, to pick up anything which has disturbed or upset people, and to become aware of where a one-to-one chat would be useful.

Putting it all together

There are eight items on the menu. How will you fit it all together? Here are two basic outlines for a ninety minute session to get you started. Coffee and chat time is not included. The rest is up to you. Remember that all timings are, and should be, approximate.

OUTLINE ONE	OUTLINE TWO
1. Introduction and welcome by group leader 5 mins 	1. Introduction and welcome by group leader 5 mins
2. Testimony 10 mins	2. Opening worship 5 mins
3. Buzz groups introducing theme for the session 10 mins	3. Buzz groups introducing theme for session 10 mins
4. Teaching input (including video) 25 mins	4. Teaching input 15 mins
5. Buzz groups with exercise/questions for discussion 15 mins	5. Group exercise/Bible Study 15 mins
6. Question and answer session 15 mins	6. Teaching input 15 mins
7. Prayer and worship 10 mins	7. Buzz groups to digest and define questions 5 mins
	8. Question and answer session 10 mins
	9. Prayer and worship 5 mins

9

Groups and learning

The way adults learn

What is taught in any group is not the same as what is learned.
The principle applies to any classroom, lecture theatre or church
service as well. Anyone called to the task of teaching the basics
of Christian faith to adults needs to take it on board.

Let's eavesdrop on a well-taught group session on the Bible.
The leader has prepared carefully. The material is good. The
session has been well structured into four short sessions of input:
one about the nature of the Bible; one about the Old Testament;
one about the New Testament; and one about personal Bible
reading. The input is broken up with group discussions and
exercises. Everyone takes part and shares honestly and openly.
But what is taught is not the same as what is learned.

Gordon, the group leader, would be very wrong to assume that
everyone has taken in, learned and understood every part of what
he has taught that night. One or two of the group will have taken
in most of what was said. One or two, perhaps, will have had
an enjoyable evening but may not be able to remember anything
they learned the next day. The rest will be somewhere in between.
A snapshot of the group, together with their "thought bubbles"
may look something like the picture overleaf.

In any group there are other factors at work in the learning
process besides the teaching content and the way the evening
is structured. As group leaders we need to understand something
about the way adults learn.

There is no such thing as the typical group — or the typical
group member. But let's invent one for now and call him Rupert.
Rupert has recently started coming to church because his wife

Figure 13

Figure 14

became a Christian and has nagged him into coming. Rather to his surprise he enjoys it and wants to learn more. He responds to the vicar's invitation to join an evangelism nurture group. The group leaders need to recognize four barriers for learning which are there in Rupert and which will affect the way he responds to the group.

Low motivation   can be one of the biggest problems in learning. It's commonly found in fourth form geography classes; church history lectures at theological college and in all kinds of church groups. In evangelism nurture groups this particular barrier to learning can be lower than at other times. Presumably people have joined the group because they believe they have something to learn. It's worth remembering, however, that the bulk of the population think that they already know all that is worth knowing about the Christian faith. It's not unlikely that at least some people will come to your group prepared to have that expectation confirmed. From time to time you will also come across the new Christian who thinks he knows it all already; has already outgrown the nursery slopes of the "basics group" and is ready to try out the ski-jump. Stand by with the ambulance and first aid kit.

Low motivation is an obvious barrier to learning anything new. If people do not want to learn then they will not be prepared to put in the effort to attend the group, to concentrate, to listen, to think and to discover. Like the other three barriers to learning, at one level low motivation in an individual or a group can be a spiritual problem to be tackled by prayer. However, two very human factors can help as well.

Remind the group that there is a lot to learn. It's important to do this every step of the way. Disciples are learners for the whole of their lives. The dynamic of becoming a Christian, for many adults, means moving from a position where you think you know everything and will learn little that's new to a position where you become a lifetime learner, eager to know more.

It helps if this emphasis on the need to learn is there in the publicity for the group and is brought out in visits to prospective group members. It sometimes helps to draw out the comparison with learning a language or learning to drive − adult experiences of learning which many people can relate to. It usually takes at least twenty driving lessons before someone takes their test. For many people it will be a lot longer. There is much more to living the Christian life than there is to driving a car.

Emphasize too that the Christian faith is an adult faith. Rupert has grown up in secular Britain. He went to Sunday School a bit and had assemblies at school. All his learning about his faith and the Bible is through the eyes of a child. He needs to discover that the Bible is an adult book and that Christianity is an adult faith. The need to learn needs to be made clear from the beginning of the group to the end so that people know, when the course comes to an end, that God's call to them is to go on learning. One of the most helpful things here can be the group leader's own willingness to go on learning in every situation.

Make it relevant. The reason people go to sleep in fourth-year geography lessons and in Church history at theological college is because they cannot see the relevance of what is being taught.

All of us have only a limited amount of energy. For most adults a great deal of that energy is already taken up with work, family and leisure commitments. If people are going to set aside time and energy to come and learn, most are going to need to see the relevance of what is being taught very quickly. If they can't see that, then attention and eventually attendance drop away.

The reason you have made it to chapter nine of this book, presumably, is because you are finding things that are relevant to your situation. No doubt the parts of the book you have learned most from are the parts which are answering the questions you are asking now. It's in those chapters that your motivation is highest and therefore your concentration is greatest.

So it's important when planning the life of the group, and especially when you are giving input, to make what you say as relevant as you can to the ordinary, everyday life of Rupert and those like him. Increasing relevance is the best way to build motivation.

Low self-esteem A teacher friend of mine once asked his first-year class the question: ''Why do you go to the chiropodist?'' A host of hands went up. Glen pointed to one boy in the centre of the class. The child was shy and a slow-learner and this was the first time he had ever put his hand up to answer one of the teacher's questions.

''Why do you go to the chiropodist, John?''

''To get my eyes tested, Sir.''

The class laughed. John never put his hand up in class again. Instead of opening up and taking part in the learning process, he closed down and went no further.

Adults are no different from children in this respect – except we don't have to be in class if we don't want to be. Rupert and most other people in our imaginary group will have low self-esteem in one or other areas of their lives. For many adults, their self-esteem will be particularly low in areas of learning and intelligence.

It can be very threatening to find yourself in the midst of a group of strangers learning about the Christian faith, particularly if you yourself feel neither learned nor articulate nor intelligent. For many people (particularly men) the fear of showing their ignorance stops them speaking, asking questions and taking part in any way in the life of the group.

One of the functions of any Christian group should be to love, to encourage and to built self-esteem in the right ways, but this should be especially the case in a group concerned with evangelism and the nurture of new Christians. People will only learn as they begin to engage with the life of the group – as they begin to talk as well as listen. People will only begin to talk as they become confident that they will not be ridiculed, shown up, seen to be ignorant or put down in any way.

"That's a bit of a stupid question, Rupert, but I'll answer it anyway," is not an appropriate response for a group leader to make – either in verbal or non-verbal language. Responses like that not only shut Rupert down – they close down the rest of the group as well. Becoming an effective group leader means learning to value every person's contribution; learning to built up the self-esteem of every group member and so ensure that more of what is taught is learned.

Low base knowledge Most people outside churches know very little about the Christian faith. If you know next to nothing about car maintenance, you will learn next to nothing from an illustrated lecture on gear drive ratios or the insides of an alternator. You are still waiting for someone to tell you, "The headlights are at the front of the car, the fuel tank is at the back and the engine is what makes the wheels turn round."

As an undergraduate I once attended what I'm sure was a fascinating talk on "The rise of anti-clericalism in nineteenth-century France". The speaker was the world's foremost expert on the subject. I learned nothing from what he said. The reason was simple: I knew (and still know) next to nothing about French history so I had no pegs to hang the new knowledge on – nowhere to store it for future reference. Because there were no pegs – nothing to relate what I was learning to what was already there – the thoughts drifted into my mind and passed straight out again. It was impossible, literally, to make any sense of them.

I suspect that for many people learning about the Christian faith in a church group it can turn into that kind of experience. Rupert's base knowledge of the faith is so low that everything except the "this is the engine" kind of talk leaves him unaffected.

It is partly for this reason that I am so uncomfortable with the approach to Christian education which is reluctant to teach anything and insists on drawing truth out of people all the time. Certainly, people need to engage in the process if learning is to happen. However, most people need, in my experience, simple, coherent, clear input about the faith which can then be related to their own lives.

This places a major responsibility on those leading to ensure the content of the teaching is right for a particular group of people. The only way to be sure of this is to obtain good, honest feedback from the sessions over a number of months. It's always easier to listen to praise rather than criticism. The people who become the most valuable teachers in a church will be the ones who allow their groups to give them negative as well as positive feedback on how they are doing.

Low level of learning skills Rupert has not been part of a structured learning situation since he left school at fifteen, and his memories of school are not very good. He has developed a number of practical learning skills through his job and life experiences. He can reflect on what is happening to him. But he finds reading difficult and hasn't read a non-fiction book in years. His concentration span is fairly short. His comprehension skills are not very great. It takes him a long time to put his thoughts into words, especially about new things. The last thing he would want to do is to express himself in writing.

No doubt Rupert, himself, would feel bad and embarrassed about all these things, if he were to be made aware of them –

as he pretty soon will be if he joins a certain type of evangelism nurture group. In such a group he may be expected to read a chapter of a book each week and comment on it; he might have to do a small group Bible study (essentially a comprehension exercise); he may be expected to listen to talks or videos lasting half an hour or more; and he may even have to take notes on a group discussion and report back from them.

Some groups may be able to cope with all of these things from week one – but many cannot and people struggle. The gates of the kingdom are effectively closed to those who do not have certain learning skills. The church's task, surely, is to take the Gospel – and to take the process of learning – to those who do not yet have those basic skills. This means, for many groups, that people will be learning how to learn as they learn about the Christian faith.

So much for the negatives of adult learning. Hopefully, a good group can go some way towards overcoming low motivation, low self-esteem and the rest. What about the positive side? Obviously Rupert will learn something from the talks and the input at group meetings. There are four other ways he will also be learning in any group. Hopefully, what he learns in these other ways will match what he learns from the content of the sessions as well.

More is "caught" than "taught"

The disciples lived with Jesus, travelled with him and saw him in every different kind of situation. No doubt being with him, they would say, was a more important kind of learning experience even than listening to him. An enquirer or new Christian will "catch" more of what it means to be a Christian from being part of any kind of group than he or she will pick up from content. The lessons learned may well be negative ("Christian men all conform, wear anoraks and never go in pubs.") or positive – about hospitality, courtesy, encouragement and love. Leading a group is about the whole person you have become in Christ – not just the way you are for two hours on a Wednesday evening.

Discovering each other

The element which lasts longest for most people in many groups are the friendships formed. Buzz groups, time spent over coffee and doing things together all help in this. People begin to share and to learn from each other. One evangelistic association published a statistic some years ago which said that each new Christian needed to find six Christian friends (not acquaintances) in the first six months of their Christian life. If that happened, the chances of them continuing in the Way were much, much greater than if it didn't. The main place such relationships will be formed is within an evangelism nurture group.

Surprising yourself

Most people, when they go home from a meeting, remember most clearly the things they have said themselves. That's why all good learning involves engagement and discussion, question and answer, commitment. Jesus asks his hearers questions over and over again: "Which of these three do you think was a neighbour to the man who fell into the hand of robbers?" It's in answering the questions that the learning takes place – not just in listening to the stories.

Surprised by God

Although Christians can learn a great deal from education theory there is always another teacher at work in Christian groups – the Holy Spirit. There is always an element of surprise in adult Christian education, too, because of the delight of working with a senior partner who knows intimately each person in each group, and who through all our stumbling and clumsiness is graciously able to lead men and women to the truth.

Building good groups

On the first night of a new course a group of complete strangers come together. You have, let's say, fifteen weeks together. Your task as leaders is to build the group into a Christian community. How does it happen?

Understanding something about the dynamics of groups helps. There are a number of different books and models which will be useful. My own favourite is the "Serendipity" model developed by Lyman Coleman.[1] The model shows four stages through which groups move on their way to Christian fellowship.

An evangelism nurture group will sometimes not move beyond the first two or three stages. Nothing is wrong in this. You simply run out of time. To illustrate all the stages let's consider the example of the church men's group. The group consisted of about twenty-five men of different ages and backgrounds, and mainly enquirers or new Christians. We met together one evening a week from April to September.

Strangers

Twenty-five men in one room on the first night. A great start. But conversation is slow. The singing goes down like a lead balloon. Conversations are slow to develop. Several admitted later that it was very nearly the first and last time they came.

This stage is self-explanatory and uncomfortable. Every new group starts here. How do you move on?

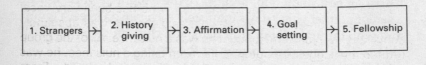

Figure 15

History-giving

Over the next four to five weeks each session begins in buzz groups. Within the small groups the men are asked to share their stories with each other. Different facts emerge about home background, work, relationships, Christian life or lack of belief. As stories are shared in the small groups — and sometimes in the larger one — the whole group begins to open up. People become people to each other — not just potential rivals, adversaries or mockers. With each part of the history-giving the atmosphere in the group lightens. People look forward to coming more. A lot of stories are retold in the pub afterwards. The group learns to laugh together. The fear has disappeared; a trust is growing in its place.

A group of strangers begin to become friends as they tell their stories to each other. As people find out more and more about each other's backgrounds then fears evaporate; confidence grows. People will be more open and willing to share with each other at a deeper level. The stories and histories which are told should not all be about faith — "testimonies" — although these help. Sharing about parents, work, children, career, home background all helps. Time invested in this aspect of history-giving at the beginning of any group repays great dividends in the weeks and months to come.

Affirmation

As the men come to know each other's stories — including some of the wounds each is carrying — they begin to share other things. Affirmation is shared next: people within the group begin to be encouraged and affirmed by individuals, or the whole group together.

At about week six or seven one man, who has been very vocal and asked a great many questions, said that he was absolutely convinced everyone else thought he was a nuisance. All of the group refuted the suggestion outright. Far from being a nuisance, he was asking the questions all the others had in their minds already. From that point on the affirmation stage of the group's life began.

History-giving needs to be structured into the group's life. Affirmation can't be structured: it just happens. Some groups are able to affirm each other very quickly. Others are much slower. Some evangelism nurture groups I have led have not come any further than history-giving. Some fellowship groups I have been part of haven't got beyond the stranger stage. When affirmation begins to happen in the group's life the leaders need to take note — it's time to think about the group moving on to stage four.

Goal-setting

"I've got so much out of this group — what are we going to do when it finishes?"

"We can't just let it die. Where else would you find so many Christian men meeting together?"

The men's group always had a deadline at which it would cease to exist — partly created by the presure of my own diary. As that deadline approached many of the men voiced a need for something to continue. Over several months that "something" was worked out — not by the group leader but by the members themselves. Different men take on the roles of hosting and leading meetings. The group itself chooses subjects. A week-end away for men has been arranged. The group has matured to the point where it can talk and share, and set goals and make decisions together.

Goal-setting, like affirmation, can't be forced. It happens at the right time. But the leaders can prepare the way and test the water from time to time, by offering the group some responsibility and/or a task to perform. Exercises can help, too. The church planting exercise, in session twelve of *Christians for Life*, is often a good indication of how far the life of the group has advanced. Doing something practical, like arranging a party or providing refreshments at a church event, is a group-building process in itself. A word of warning: once a group has reached the goal-setting stage of its life you may find it very difficult, if not impossible, to disband.

Fellowship

On the penultimate night of the scheduled men's group one man put it into words for many of us:

"I can honestly say, without embarrassment, that I love the members of this group."

By the grace of God, members of the group are able to laugh together, cry together, walk together, pray together, love each other and care for each other. New people can come into the group and take part in the fellowship. Others can drop out for a while and then come back. When that group of people gets together now something special happens – Christian fellowship.

Real fellowship, community and friendship are all too rare – even in Christian circles. All good fruit takes time to mature. If ever a group in your care grows to that point, without turning inwards, treasure it and thank God for it. The blessings will be very great.

Ground rules and agendas

Ground rules help groups grow. With clear ground rules people know where they stand. The expectations of the leaders and of the church are clear. Everything is out in the open and above board. Advance notice of ground rules can be given in the publicity for the course but the best time and place to explain them is on the first night.

These are the ones we have developed:

GROUND RULES FOR AN EVANGELISM NURTURE GROUP
1. Please follow the course through and come every week: continuity and commitment are important.
2. Please let someone know if you can't come on a particular day.
3. Please be punctual. We start at 8.00 p.m. and aim to finish the content of the meeting by 9.45 p.m.

4. Please be honest. Everything the leaders say is based on conviction and honesty. Be honest in your views and questions, and in your comments as we go along.

5. Please contribute as and when you want to. No one will be "singled out" and asked to read aloud, or answer a question, or contribute to a discussion. It's up to you how much you say or whether you remain quiet.

I have found that people respond well to high expectations about attendance and punctuality. Where nothing is said, bad habits can take over. The group is important and the life of it suffers if people become casual about coming or arrive late. It's better for them not to have come in the first place than to be half-hearted.

The agenda for the group should also be clear. Hopefully it will be clear from the initial publicity: that the purpose of the group is to enable people to find out more about the Christian faith and to lay a firm foundation for belief and practice. It's worth restating that at the initial meeting. The vast majority of people are honest and take a group at face value. Occasionally you will find people bring hidden agendas with them and try and hijack the group in their own direction. It's on those occasions you need to remember that a leader is there to lead. If necessary, have a word with the person outside the meeting and uncover what lies behind the move.

Handling problems

Groups are not full of problem people. It would be wrong to give that impression. Most people simply want to come and learn and grow in the Christian life. But from time to time deeper problems will surface in people's lives. Sometimes they will break to the surface during a group meeting. Usually they will need to be dealt

Figure 16

with outside the group – that means spending time with people on their own.

Every group leader also needs someone to talk to about the group: someone to bounce ideas off; ask for help; analyse what is happening. Co-leaders can be a good support here, so can the minister. Some form of reflection is essential. Group leaders are people too . . .

Note to chapter 9

1.   Lyman Coleman, *Search the Scripture* (London: Scripture Union, 1983).

10

Making a commitment to Christ

"I listened to what Tim said in the service, about asking God into your life. I just knew that was what I needed and so I asked him in. All my heaviness just lifted. I felt warm all over. I just want to learn more and be more committed now." (Dawn)

"I got home after my first visit to church and I began washing my week's dirty dishes. I started smiling and laughing to myself, then all of a sudden things just seemed brighter. The light, coming in through the windows, came and hit me in the face and I started shaking with happiness, shivers ran down my arms and up my back and almost out through the back of my head as though someone had their hand on me. I knew something had happened and I had to get back to church that evening. I talked to Hillarie afterwards and she told me that the Holy Spirit had come to me." (Tony)

"I left Steve's house some time later greatly encouraged, refreshed in body and spirit. In my hand I carried a copy of *Journey Into Life*. That night, having achieved a suitable state of mind, I asked Christ to come into my life. I did this with considerable apprehension, as my life had been sinful and I had ignored his presence for many years. I feared rejection and yet so desperately wanted him. The response was immediate and a feeling of utter peace swept over my whole being and totally filled the room. I read my Bible and spent the happiest night I had experienced in many years." (Ken)

"After we'd been coming to church for some time we asked Jesus into our lives and prayed a prayer of commitment, and now we let him take control of our lives." (Paul and Sue)

Although becoming a Christian is a process, not an event, for most people there is still a moment of decision; of commitment; of surrender; of rebirth. Different churches and spiritual traditions use different words – rightly so. We are trying, in one sense, to describe the indescribable: God's work in human hearts and lives. Some people are able to communicate a part of what they experience. For others, it remains a part of them which is too deep for words: a private experience of joy.

Those of us called to lead groups for evangelism and nurture need to have an understanding of this process of commitment. We also need to know how to assist and guide at this point in a person's Christian life.

Explaining commitment to a group

How do we explain Christian commitment to those who are ready to learn? How do we assist someone through the process of becoming a Christian? This is one subject where the practical needs to come before any theory. We are going to listen in on an evangelism nurture group which is following the Christians for Life syllabus. This is week six of the course.

The group consists of fifteen people, including the three leaders. The sessions have focused so far upon God's existence; upon our need of God; on Jesus' ministry, death and resurrection; and on the Holy Spirit. The aim of session six is to tie all of this together and give a clear invitation to commitment to Christ.

The leaders are aware that several members in the group have already made a commitment in some form. One or two have been part of the church for many years and this language may be new to them. A few others are still asking questions and are not at all ready to declare themselves Christians.

The group assembles to start at 8.00 p.m. The meeting is in the home of one of the co-leaders. Jenny, the group leader, welcomes everyone formally and opens with a short prayer.

"It's good to see you all again tonight. We've just had apologies from Bill, who has had to work late. Hopefully he'll be along later on.

"As we said last week, tonight is a very important session of the course, where we try and pull together everything that has gone on over the last six weeks. What's involved in becoming a Christian? As normal, we're going to break into small groups to begin with. The questions are on the sheet. As always, don't feel you have to say anything you don't want to – but please be as honest as you can."

(Chapter continues on p. 176)

Sharing your story

Share the story of your journey to faith. Are you a Christian? How did you come to faith?

Can you say what is wrong with these descriptions of what a Christian is?

* I went to Sunday School
* I'm as good as him
* I believe in God
* We were married in church
* I enjoy "Songs of Praise"
* I was baptized as a baby
* I'm not anything else
* My wife goes

How would you describe a Christian?

The room is a buzz of conversation. Jenny sits back and gets a perspective on what is happening and how the buzz groups are developing. After about ten minutes, with some difficulty, she draws people together. There is a whole group discussion around the "wrong descriptions" of the Christian life which leads naturally into Jenny's second input.

"Thanks for sharing so honestly there. I think all of us begin to see the difficulty we have in our society now. Just because of our history many people all around us believe themselves to be Christians. But most people who believe themselves to be Christians have only begun to understand what the Christian faith is about. They may pray from time to time, and go to church on special occasions, but that's about it.

"That simply isn't the picture of Christianity we have found in the New Testament over these last weeks. It isn't the kind of discipleship that Jesus calls us to. Being a Christian is not something vague — it's something definite. You know when you are a Christian. Being a Christian is not something private. It is a public thing. Jesus makes it clear he expects us to stand up and be counted. He also expects us to play our part in his church — not stand aloof from it.

"No one is born a Christian. It's something which makes Christianity different from other faiths. You may be born into a Christian family, and it can be a great help if you are. But each person has to make their own decision to follow Christ as they grow.

"No one becomes a Christian by accident either. You become a Christian by making a deliberate decision to follow Jesus Christ. Jesus calls us to a whole-hearted commitment to him. He calls this whole process of committing your life to him being born again."

Jenny goes on to give a brief and simple outline of the Gospel, based on the hand-out. At every point she refers the group back to the teaching in previous sessions.

After the outline of the Gospel the group again spends some time in threes, checking that people understand what has been said and giving a chance to ask any questions. One or two of the questions are dealt with when the group comes back together, before Jenny continues with her presentation.

"As we've said over the weeks, for most people becoming a Christian is a process which may take months, sometimes years. For others it will seem faster than that. But we are all different. God

The Christian Gospel

1. GOD'S LOVE

God made us.
He loves us.
He wants the best for us.

2. OUR NEED

We were created to know God.
Be we have turned away from him.
We have rejected his love.
We are sinners.

3. JESUS

God sent his son, Jesus, to draw us back to him.
Jesus lived a life without sin.
He died on the cross. God raised him from the dead.
Through Jesus, God offers to everyone:
forgiveness of sins
a new relationship with God
the gift of eternal life.

4. OUR RESPONSE

We need to make a response to God's offer — to his grace.
Our response is fourfold:
repentance
faith
becoming a full member of the church
receiving the promised gift of the Holy Spirit.

deals with us as individuals — he doesn't process us along a conveyor belt.

"The process is like a journey back to God — remember that we spent some time thinking about the journey of the younger son in week two. We said then that there are several significant points on the journey. Wanting to know more is one such point — most of you have come to that stage otherwise you wouldn't be part of this group. Finding out about Christianity is another — that's what we've been doing in the course so far. Sensing your own need of God is another. I know from what's been said that some people find they have reached that point. Others in the group have some difficulty there.

"And a fourth significant point on the journey, the one we have focused on this evening, is making a commitment to follow Christ. For everyone who looks seriously into the Christian faith there comes a moment of decision and commitment. It's the time when you stop calling yourself an enquirer and begin to call yourself a Christian.

"Some of you may already have made that commitment before you joined this group. Others, perhaps, have made it over the last few weeks. But there will be some here who have never made an act of commitment to follow Christ, so we're going to take some time to explain what's involved.

"You may want to make a commitment (or recommitment) to Christ at this point in time because you know this is the right time for you to come back to God; because your understanding and faith are deeper now than when you first became a Christian; or because you want to be filled with the Holy Spirit in a new and deeper way.

"A commitment to Christ is made through prayer, either on your own or with someone else. There are lots of different prayers you can use — or just put it in your own words. But one way of praying is given on tonight's sheet. You can say the prayers there on your own. Take some time to prepare and to be quiet before God and use either your own words or the ones on the sheet.

"Many people find it better to meet with one or two people who are already Christians and to make that act of commitment with their prayer and support. It's especially helpful — and biblical — for other Christians to pray for us to be filled with the Holy Spirit.

"If you're at the point in your own journey where you want to make that act of commitment, then I or the other group leaders will be very happy to meet with you in the next couple of weeks, and to go through these prayers with you.

"Then in due course you will be received into full membership of the church by baptism and confirmation (or just confirmation if you were baptized as a child). At that point you will make a public profession of faith using some of the same words in the prayer.

"Let's read the prayer through together, pausing at each stage, and thinking about what it means."

Jenny goes through the prayer carefully. She emphasizes the fourfold structure of repentance, faith, membership of the church (expressed by baptism) and being filled with the Holy Spirit. The group is referred to the end of Peter's sermon in Acts 2:

"Repent and be baptized, every one of you, in the name of Jesus Christ for the forgiveness of your sins. And you will receive the gift of the Holy Spirit." Acts 2:38

As she outlines the importance of repentance Jenny is careful to stress that the forgiveness God offers is complete: that no sin is too great to be forgiven; that it is best to be as specific as possible when naming your sins before God; that repentance means turning from everything you know is wrong.

As she talks through belief Jenny talks about the importance of faith and of trusting in God in the Christian life. Our whole life is placed in his love now.

As she talks through service and membership of the church Jenny stresses the cost of Christian commitment, the joy of being part of God's family and the way God's plans for us are always, in the end, the best way.

And as she talks about receiving the Holy Spirit Jenny encourages the group to allow God to do what he wants to do. For some people there will be a dramatic experience of God's presence and love, perhaps accompanied by new spiritual gifts. For other people there will be no obvious, immediate change at that point — but another milestone on the journey.

The group ends with another brief discussion on advice for new Christians. Right at the end of the session Jenny leads the group in a time of silent prayer: each responding to God in her or his own way. The offer to pray through a prayer of commitment sometime during the week is made again and coffee is served.

AN ACT OF COMMITMENT TO CHRIST

A prayer of repentance

Before you pray, pause and bring to mind all of the things you want to say sorry for and turn from.

Heavenly Father,
I thank you for your love for me.

I have sinned against you and against others,
In what I have thought and said and done.
I have rebelled against you and gone my own way.
I am sorry and ashamed and I ask for your forgiveness.

I turn to Christ.
I repent of my sins.
I renounce evil.

Be assured that your sins are now forgiven through Jesus (1 John 1:8—9). If others are praying with you, they should pronounce God's forgiveness (James 5:16).

A confession of faith

I believe and trust in God the Father, who made the world.
I believe and trust in his Son, Jesus Christ, who redeemed mankind.
I believe and trust in his Holy Spirit, who gives life to the people of God.

A promise to serve and to be part of God's Church

I give my life to you.
I will follow you with my whole heart.
I will serve you faithfully as a member of your Church.

An invitation to Christ to come and live in your life and fill you with his Holy Spirit

Come, Lord Jesus, now and live in my life.
Fill me with your Holy Spirit,
strengthen me for your service
and empower me with your love.
Amen.

Those praying with you should now lay hands upon you and pray that God will fill you with his Holy Spirit.

Praying with people on their own

Jenny and her co-leaders end up praying with four of the group members in the fortnight that follows the session described above. Three others in the group know clearly where they stand and don't feel they need a session on their own (although Jenny does ask them). One person drops out of the group at this point, saying she has realized that Christianity is not for her. Two make a quiet act of commitment on their own and talk it through with the leaders afterwards. Two are still undecided and have lots of questions.

Christine is in her early fifties and a very quiet member of the group. Her faith has gradually been growing stronger through the last few months. Jenny is quite surprised when Christine approaches her and asks if she can go round and pray, but they arrange to meet one afternoon. Pauline, one of the co-leaders comes too.

After a cup of tea and a brief chat, Jenny asks Christine to tell them "the story so far" and what she would like to pray through today. Christine outlines the story of her life and faith. It takes some time and patient listening. She had a Christian childhood. In early adult life she knew God was calling her to serve him in some special way, but the distractions came and she wandered away. For years she has convinced herself that she is really a Christian – but the group has helped her realize that she needs to start again and to ask God's forgiveness for the wasted years. Only she's not really sure that he will take her back and she is very afraid of letting him down again.

Pauline and Jenny take time to assure Christine about these last points. Together they look at some Bible references about assurance of God's love, the strength the Holy Spirit gives, and the importance of Christian fellowship. One or two other questions come to light and are answered.

Christine is ready then to pray. It seems appropriate to kneel together, so the three kneel down on the living room floor. Pauline invites Christine to say "sorry" first of all. Christine isn't very good at praying aloud and so she names all of the things she wants to say in her mind to God, saying "Amen" aloud when she has finished. Then she prays aloud the prayer of repentance on the sheet. Pauline assures her in very simple words, based on the Scriptures, that all her sins are now forgiven and she is washed clean.

Christine now places her trust in Christ completely, using the words from the sheet, spoken aloud. Commitment to the Church comes next. Jenny emphasizes the great need Christine has to develop a good discipline of worship (so far that's been a bit shaky). Christine acknowledges that she needs to get that sorted out and she then prays through the third part of the prayer.

Last of all, with Jenny and Pauline kneeling beside her, Christine invites God to come into her life. Jenny and Pauline lay hands on her and pray for her to be filled with the Holy Spirit. A deep sense of peace fills the room.

Hugs follow – so does another cup of tea. Jenny and Pauline spend a little while longer with Christine, assuring her of the reality of what has happened and encouraging her in the new beginning. The three agree to meet again at the group in a couple of days' time.

Tom's experience is very different. He knows God is doing something in his life, but he doesn't know what. He began the group with all kinds of questions. Most of them have been answered. He still doesn't "feel" anything – in fact he's very sceptical about all this talk of feelings. He agrees when Donald, the other co-leader, suggests he comes round for a chat and prayers. The two of them spend an evening talking together, with Jenny there as well.

After an hour's hard talking Tom acknowledges that he has no more questions left. He does want to believe, but he doesn't feel anything inside. He could never be like the others. And he's frightened about what the people at work will say. Donald explains very gently that Tom is at a crossroads. He does have a real choice to make. Will he go forward in faith with Christ? or will he turn away? Tom makes his choice and he is ready to pray.

Once again, the team lead Tom through the act of commitment, stage by stage: repentance; faith; a promise to serve and be part of the Church; an invitation to Christ to come into Tom's life. It's all very unemotional stuff. It takes Donald all his courage to lay hands on Tom at the end and pray for him to be filled with the Spirit. Nothing dramatic happens at all. Donald and Jenny stay and talk for a while and then leave, fealing weak and vulnerable and afraid they might have messed it up. But over the weeks that follow Tom grows more confident in the group. His faith is becoming stronger. At his confirmation he gives a clear testimony before the whole congregation, thanking Donald and Jenny for coming to pray with him that night. It really helped him come off the fence.

Mavis has been a Christian for many years but, like the disciples in Ephesus (Acts 19:2), has never been taught about the Holy Spirit. After the group session on the Spirit and spiritual gifts Mavis has a hunger inside to go deeper with God. At her request, Donald and Pauline meet with her for prayer. They spend time listening to where she is and then lead her through an act of recommitment and dedication to Christ. At the end, once again, they lay their hands on her and pray for her to be filled with the Spirit. Mavis later describes how she felt a warm sensation through her body. Strange words began to come into her mind. She spoke them out and was more surprised when Pauline assured her she was speaking in tongues. More important even than the tongues, over the next few weeks Mavis opened up to God and to others: her faith had much more vitality; prayer and Bible reading were no longer chores; and she began to seek opportunities to share her faith at work.

The last person the team were asked to pray with was Stanley. Stanley, like the others, knew he was ready to make an act of commitment. But there was a barrier there and he knew it. Five years previously Stanley's wife had run off with another man. Ever since that day he had been bitter and estranged from his ex-wife and from his grown-up children. He had tried asking God into his life before but he knew there could be no whole-hearted commitment without forgiveness. ''It's there in the Lord's Prayer,'' he told Donald, '' 'forgive us our sins as we forgive those who sin against us.' ''

Donald and Jenny didn't pray with Stanley the evening they talked. They felt out of their depth. But they arranged for Stanley to have some time with the vicar. The vicar listened to Stanley's story and talked through with him the nature of forgiveness, and the damage the bitterness was doing to his life. In the end, in the vicar's study, Stanley let go of all the hurt and invited God into his life. Instantly he knew things were different. The months to come were to prove him right.

There is no such thing as a "typical" prayer of commitment. Every one of us is different. The person involved in this ministry will find, over and over again, that the most important thing we can do is really to listen to what people are saying. We can then, by God's grace, help them to pray in an appropriate way. Listening takes time. That's why it's essential that these conversations about Christian commitment and the prayers take place outside of services and meetings, in a place where there is no pressure and no time constraint.

Some questions and answers

Why is there a fourfold process? Does it need to be that complicated?

To answer the second question first — it doesn't "need" to be complicated at all. The whole process of conversion and commitment is God's work. There are no set formulas which are right on every occasion. The Lord knows what is in a person's heart, whatever words are used or prayers are prayed. If you have a "favourite" prayer of commitment, which God has honoured and used in your situation, stay with it.

However, it is surely right that our theology of conversion and models of commitment should spring from New Testament theology and practice as closely as possible. There is no simple "sinner's prayer" given in the Bible. Through all of the different accounts of conversion, however, four elements are present:

repentance; faith; baptism in water (signifying membership of the Church); and being filled with the Holy Spirit.[1] It has to be said that the most commonly used prayers of commitment are largely based on a single verse in Revelation (3:20) — a verse which is, in any case, addressed to those who are already Christians. A broader, New Testament base is better.

The fourfold structure to the act of commitment has the merit of drawing out the theology and stressing each element clearly. For some people one will be more important than another at a particular time. It takes the emphasis away from "saying the magic words" and places it firmly upon an attitude of heart, mind and life. The new Christian can be taken step-by-step through each stage of the prayer, stopping along the way for explanation, questions and encouragement.

Finally, an act of commitment has real links with the life, practice and liturgy of the church. A new relationship with others is emphasized as well as a new relationship with God. There is a clear link between the words of the prayer and the services of baptism, confirmation and the renewal of baptismal vows; and between the words of the prayer and the on-going liturgy of the Christian community.

What about "baptism" in the Holy Spirit?

The Church of England and other mainstream denominations have rediscovered the Holy Spirit over the last thirty years. That rediscovery, in the movement we now call the Charismatic Renewal, came via the Pentecostal churches. It has taken time for theology to catch up with experience in the Renewal movement. The result of this is that there is widespread confusion over terms like "baptism in the Holy Spirit", over the gift of the Holy Spirit, and over spiritual gifts.

It is important that clear teaching on all of these points is given in the local church context. Five points need to be made clear:

The Holy Spirit is at work in every Christian. Paul writes that no one can say "Jesus is Lord" except by the Holy Spirit (1

Corinthians 12:3). The New Testament will not allow a division between Christians who have the Holy Spirit and those who have not – apart from the two exceptional cases of new disciples in Samaria and in Ephesus. The Holy Spirit is active in the life of every believer. To say otherwise is to divide the Church.

The Spirit's work in each person's life will be different. The whole emphasis of Paul's teaching on the Holy Spirit is that there is one Spirit and one Church, but that the Holy Spirit works in different ways in each member of the Church. The Corinthian Christians (and some of their present-day followers) argue that there is one Spirit and he works in the same way in every Christian – so there cannot be one Church.

We love to put things into neat boxes but our neat theologies cannot contain the Holy Spirit. We need simply to allow God to do what he wants to do in our lives and in his Church.

There is a definite experience of baptism in the Spirit. The New Testament speaks of this experience. Many people know it today. The Greek word *baptizo* means, very simply, "to drench". From time to time in our lives, and in the life of his Church, God will pour out the Holy Spirit in very large measure, all at once. It is right, on those occasions, to describe the experience as a real drenching, a baptism in the Holy Spirit.

Some people will receive such a "drenching" at or near their conversion. For some it will occur years later: perhaps after a time of dryness in their Christian life; perhaps as God's anointing for a particular piece of ministry. For some people there may well be several "drenchings".

In others, God will work in a different way. In many people, both conversion and being filled with the Spirit happen gradually and slowly over a long period of time. When people ask me if I have been "baptized" with the Spirit I often (a little mischievously) say "No". That's because my own experience of God has been a "dripping" rather than a "drenching". There have been many, many times of experiencing the refreshing rain of the Spirit; many times of experiencing God's empowering; but no single time I am happy to call a "drenching". Perhaps that's still to come. I hope it is.

The Spirit's work will be continual.   The disciples are baptized with the Holy Spirit in Acts 2. Later they are found praying together in Acts 4. "After they prayed," Luke writes, "the place where they were meeting was shaken. And they were all filled with the Holy Spirit and spoke the word of God boldly." Acts 4:31 Just a minute – I thought that had already happened two chapters ago. It did. But God then fills them again and again and again as they seek his blessing and reach out in ministry.

Paul writes to the Christians in Ephesus: "Don't keep on getting drunk with wine; go on being filled with the Spirit;" (Ephesians 5:18; author's translation.) We keep on drying out so we need to keep on being refreshed. The important thing is not the experiences you have had in the past, it is what you are experiencing of God's presence and power today.

The gifts of the Holy Spirit are for today.   As we pray for new Christians to receive the Holy Spirit, he will come and bring spiritual gifts. Good teaching on how to use the gifts will be needed. They are tools not toys – vital for the health and up-building of Christian lives and of the Church. Paul teaches very clearly that the gift of tongues is no different from all of the other gifts: it is given to *some* Christians (1 Corinthians 12:30). It should not be made into some kind of sign that a person has genuinely received the Holy Spirit, as in the Pentecostal churches and some Charismatic teaching.

We can reject God's blessing for us.   The New Testament speaks of the Holy Spirit being resisted (Acts 7:1), grieved (Ephesians 4:30), deserted (Galatians 3:3), insulted (Hebrews 10:29) and ignored (Revelation 2:7).

It is our responsibility to lead new Christians into every blessing that God has for them, to give clear teaching and to point the way. Leading people into a full experience of God's presence and power through the Holy Spirit is a vital part of that work.

Who is sufficient for these things?

It is a great privilege and responsibility to draw alongside someone as they make an act of commitment to Christ. Every spiritual birth, like every natural birth, is different. I was greatly blessed to be present at the birth of each of my four children. It was a humbling and deeply joyful experience each time, although my part in the proceedings was limited. Being present at a spiritual birth produces the same feelings. This is God's work. We are there to encourage and help where we can – not to get in the way.

The enemy will do all he can to disrupt and upset this aspect of our ministry of growing Christians. We need to be bold and to be encouraged, and to remember it is God who gives the growth.

Note to chapter 10

1. A very significant book on the theology of conversion is David Pawson's *The Normal Christian Birth* (London: Hodder and Stoughton, 1989). As an Anglican, I disagree with David Pawson on infant baptism but find a broad measure of agreement with his theology in other areas.

11

The pastoral care of new Christians

The parable of the sower

"A farmer went out to sow his seed . . ." Luke 8:5

Of all the stories Jesus tells, the parable of the sower might have been told especially for leaders of evangelism nurture groups. Above all other ministries in Church we need to learn that not every seed that is sown bears fruit. Many will drop out along the way. That was the experience of Jesus and of Paul. It is certain to be ours.

My main responsibility as a curate was the care of a medium-size youth group. Each year we would take the group for a week-end away. One particular year we did so almost in despair. The majority of the group seemed further away from becoming Christians than ever before. We had just had a town-wide youth mission. The young people had more or less completely disowned it. Looking back now I can understand why. It was hard to get anything serious going at all.

A great deal of prayer went into the week-end. A friend of mine came to be our speaker, with a team from his church. On the Saturday evening he spoke very simply and powerfully about the cross and invited people to raise their hands if they would like to make a commitment to Christ. About six of the young people did so. You can perhaps imagine our joy as we prayed with each of the six that evening. The speaker and his team left us on the Saturday night. It seemed to everyone as though the main event of the week-end had happened.

Then on the Sunday morning, at the end of a very low-key service of Holy Communion, God began to move in power through the group. One by one almost the whole group was touched by the Holy Spirit. There were tears and hugs on the outside and in many cases deep changes taking place on the inside. For some, it was an experience of a faith they had had for a long time, coming alive. For others, coming to faith for the first time. Others could not put the experience into words. The following week twenty-seven teenagers out of a total group of thirty-five took part in Bible study groups. Parents reported radical changes for the better in their offspring. It was a new beginning for the group and in many lives.

Over the months that followed, we were able to see the parable of the sower in action in the life of each of the young people. For one or two, the experience was easily shrugged off. At that time, the Word of God bounced off them like seed off a drum. The devil snatched away what had been sown in their hearts and there was no beginning and no fruit.

Others made a good start. Church attendance went up. They came to Bible study groups. New qualities began to form in their lives. Then the time of testing came. Friends began to mock. In some cases there was no support from families. The feelings began to fade. Their new Christian life which had started so well became hard-going. Like the seed on the rock they believed for a while, but in the time of testing, fell away.

It's vital to realize that the time of testing will come for every new Christian. It's a very common thing for the Christian life to begin with great joy: walking on cloud nine; joy inside; new friends outside; a new sense of purpose and of peace; dramatic answers to prayer.

It is also a very common thing – although sadly many new Christians are not prepared for it – for this time of joy to be followed by a time of testing. A bit of persecution comes at work or at home. Something goes badly wrong in life. Where was God then? The feelings begin to fade. Perhaps someone in the church is rude or unkind. Perhaps you stay away for a week and no one seems to notice.

New Christians can be greatly helped by being prepared for this to happen. It's good to enjoy the "up" times of any Christian life. But it is vital to know that the hard times will come. And that it is often in those hard times that the real Christian virtues are forged. It is also very important to stay close to new Christians so that you know when they are passing through the hard times and can be there to help them through. For those whose conversion and change of life has not been dramatic or sudden, the hard times may not be so sudden either. But for those who have experienced a dramatic conversion the time of testing may come without warning, very quickly. Good pastoring means anticipating that this may happen and staying close enough to do something about it.

A third group of our young people kept going through the initial time of testing and grew stronger for it. As enthusiasm and emotion ebbed, good disciplines of worship, prayer, fellowship and learning took their place. There was still a need for a high level of support. Then the thorns began to grow up in their lives. Boyfriends and parties, for some, became more important than seeking the kingdom. For others it was schoolwork. For others, less wholesome aspects of the teenage lifestyle. One by one, they fell away.

"The seed which fell among thorns stands for those who hear, but as they go on their way they are choked by life's worries, riches and pleasures and they do not mature." Luke 8:14

The parable of the sower is the saddest of the parables, because it is so true. Over and over again we see thorns growing up and choking the life out of the seed. Jesus is quite specific about what the thorns are: life's worries, riches and pleasures. For many new, adult Christians they will include: working long hours to be better-off financially, but squeezing out time for worship and fellowship; hobbies which intrude and take up a person's prime time; the caravan club in summer which can effectively take a person out of the church for months at a time; the list is endless.

Those of us caring for new Christians need to give a clear warning here. The seed that has taken root in the person's life may seem very strong to them but in reality it is still a delicate plant. It may one day grow so that it is the largest of the trees in the garden and cannot be uprooted so easily. But in this early stage, especially, it needs to be kept free of weeds and thorns. Encourage people to do their own weeding where they can. Don't be afraid, either, to point out the weeds when you see them. I have had to learn some honesty and bluntness here. It's much more comfortable (and much less embarrassing) if you see a weed growing in someone's life to pray that it goes away, or to pray that they realize what is happening. We are called to keep watch over each other, however. Sometimes that means speaking bluntly and telling someone if a hobby or practice is putting their whole Christian life in danger. If they will listen, well and good. If they refuse, at least the warning has been given.

The fourth group from our youth week-end was the largest — although that is not always the case. It's now seven years since our week-end away. Many of the young people on that week-end are still active, young, adult, Christian disciples: a nurse; a teacher; a housing officer; a driving instructor; a children's entertainer; a designer; an ordinand. Many are active still in the life of their own or other churches: as youth leaders; Sunday School teachers; home group leaders; musicians. There has been a great deal of input for all of them since that week-end away, in different church contexts. Some, doubtless, will look back now and not see that particular week-end as very significant at all. Others would see it as very important. "But the seed on good soil stands for those with a noble and good heart, who hear the word, retain it, and by persevering produce a crop." Luke 8:15

It takes time for new Christians to grow to maturity. All will pass through times of testing and times when the weeds grow. Special care is needed from those called to work in the harvest field.

Barriers to growth

"My Christian life got off to such a good start, but I just don't seem to be making any head-way now . . ."

If you are keeping an eye on the members of your group, during the group's life and in the six months to a year afterwards, the chances are that you will have a number of conversations which begin in that way.

Besides the times of testing and the thorns, there are a number of other barriers to Christian growth which at different times can stop a person moving forward in discipleship. Each needs dealing with in a different way. I have identified the five most common barriers. You may be able to think of others.

Sin and lifestyle

Sin is an old-fashioned word and sometimes an unpopular one. It's also the most common cause of a person not moving foward with God.

When a person comes to Christ, all of our sins are forgiven. We do not become perfect. There may well be several large areas of our life and lifestyle which God does not set right immediately. However, over the first months and years of our Christian lives he will begin to work on these things. The timing needs to be his, not the church's.

A very common situation is when a person becomes a Christian and they are not married, but living with a partner, possibly the couple have a child or children. Very commonly, the children may not have the same father. In God's timing, those relationships rarely seem to be a barrier to faith initially. A person will come right into the heart of the church and often through a Christians for Life group (where clear teaching on Christian morality is given) without feeling specifically challenged in this area.

But at some point God will begin to set this area right – certainly before the person can engage in any significant ministry in the church's life. It is at that point that the person may well face very difficult choices about their lifestyle. That's when all the love, help and guidance the church can provide is needed. We do people no favours, in the long term, by diluting Christian teaching about marriage or sexual standards. Yet that teaching needs to be applied with love, without judging, and with pastoral sensitivity to each person and situation.

Even where relationships are outwardly "in order", when a

Figure 17

person becomes a Christian as an adult there will be many areas of sin remaining to be dealt with. A very high proportion of adults will have been involved with pornography and sexual immorality of different kinds, including extra-marital affairs. After the first few months of a person's Christian life these things may well surface again, as the Holy Spirit continues his work, and need dealing with before growth can continue. Others are involved in dishonest practices at work. Others will be trapped by ambition or greed. I have known several people who have been compulsive liars to different degrees after they have made very sincere professions of Christian faith.

One lesson, in my own experience, is that new Christians who are being blocked in their growth by sin in their lives will very often be critical and judgemental in their attitude to the church and other Christians. We do not want to face our own guilt, so we project it onto others. We do not want to see the beam in our own eye, so we find the speck in our brother's.

Sin needs dealing with in a comprehensive way, first of all by clear teaching and then through prayer. "Confess your sins to each other and pray for each other so that you may be healed," writes James (James 5:16). If it is sin which is blocking Christian growth, it often helps to confess that sin aloud to another Christian, preferably someone with a recognized ministry in the church. The sin is brought to the cross. It's power is broken. Counsel about the future can be given and the Christian is able to go forward.

Past hurt

Revelation 3:20 gives the beautiful picture of the believer asking Jesus into his or her life, and sitting down to eat. The picture is of a life being like a house. To extend the picture, it is as though there are many rooms in the house. For most of us, the house is very run-down and dilapidated when we ask the Lord in. He doesn't leave it that way and sets to work cleaning, mending and remaking. He does this gently and in his own time, and it is a process which will last for the whole of our lives.

As part of that work, he will go down into the cellars and up into the attics and open doors which we have kept closed for many years. Hurts from the past will be brought to the surface. For years we have pushed them down, locked them away and thrown the key away. The Holy Spirit begins to bring them out into the light so that, in his love, they can be mended and healed.

Again, the new Christian and the pastor need to have an understanding of that process. All of us carry hurt with us from the past. In some cases it is very deep hurt indeed: sexual and physical abuse; rejection; abandonment; breakdown in relationships; the list is almost endless. In God's time much of that hurt can be healed. Generally speaking, this is not a process which begins immediately you become a Christian. But a church which is finding a lot of people coming to faith will need to become equipped in ministering to these past hurts, through counselling and what has become known as the ministry of inner healing. Jesus is the one who comes to bind up the broken hearted (Isaiah 60:2). Often he will call us to aid him in that work.

There is not the space here to unpack all that is involved in this particular ministry. There are a number of good books available for those who want to learn more.[1] Nor is it necessary for every evangelism nurture group leader to be able to deal with these hurts as they come up. But the group leader does need to be able to recognize what may be happening and to refer the person to someone else in the church for help.

Unforgiveness

If there has been past hurt of any kind, there will almost always be unforgiveness. Paul and Sue were part of a Christians for Life group two years ago. When Wendy, the co-leader, and I met to pray with them as they committed their lives to Christ, unforgiveness was a barrier to both of them. Sue had been badly hurt by a former colleague. She knew that if she became a Christian that resentment would have to go. Paul had been estranged from his father for several years. There had been a family quarrel. Both were proud men. Neither would make the first move.

Sue's barrier was so strong it needed to come down before she could honestly come to Christ. We talked through what it means to forgive and to hand the situation to God. We prayed for the strength for Sue to forgive. Eventually, in prayer, she was able to say from the heart: "Lord, I forgive this person." The barrier was down. Sue was able to make a full commitment to Christ.

Paul didn't find his broken relationship with his father a barrier initially. His Christian life began with great joy and enthusiasm. Then, in the first three or four months, God began to nudge Paul about his dad at every opportunity. Paul struggled and wrestled and fought. In the end, he gave in. He made the first move. The quarrel was ended and the three generations in the family were reunited.

Forgiveness is almost always the key to releasing inner hurt and enabling the healing to take place. Once again, the leader of a group may not be the best person to pray through these difficulties – but in some instances you may well find you are the best person for the task.

If you find yourself in that position, the following guidelines may be useful.

- As with all other pastoral situations, listen first. Don't jump to conclusions about the problem. Take the trouble to listen properly to what the person says.
- It's important for the person to understand Jesus' teaching on the importance of forgiveness (Matthew 6:9–15; 18:21–35) and the damage that bitterness can do.
- Unforgiveness, at its root, is the desire for revenge and to hurt. To forgive means handing the matter over to God and allowing his justice to prevail (Romans 12:17–21).
- To say "I forgive you" is not the same as saying "What you did to me doesn't matter – let's forget about it." To say "I forgive you" means to say: "What you did to me was terrible. It hurt me very deeply and has had serious consequences for

my life, and for other people. But because Jesus has forgiven me, I choose to forgive you now.''

- To forgive is, usually, something between the person and God, and need not involve any specific renewed contact with the person who has caused the offence. It is quite possible for people to hold a strong resentment against someone who has died, and it is still possible – and a very good thing – for that resentment to be released.
- To forgive is a matter of the will, not the emotions. If the will is rightly aligned, emotions and feelings will follow.
- Often, when praying, people find it very difficult to say aloud the words: "Father, I forgive 'x'." Other forms of words come out instead such as, "Father, help me to forgive 'x' " or "Father, I really want to forgive 'x' " or "Father, I'm really trying to forgive 'x'." To say these things is not to forgive. You may need to keep explaining this and to go back through the prayer until the bitterness is released.[2]

Occult involvement

There has been an explosion of interest in occult phenomena during the last twenty-five years. Taking part in seances, playing with Ouija boards and a fascination with all kinds of paranormal phenomena are commonplace among adults in Britain. A good number of those who are becoming Christians from secular backgrounds will have had some kind of occult involvement in the past.

Sometimes all the consequences of that involvement will be dealt with by God, in his own way: without any fuss; in the normal process of becoming a Christian; through the life of the group; and through baptism and confirmation. It's not necessary for everyone who has dabbled in these things to go through a specific ritual of renunciation. But it will be necessary for some. If it is, you will be able to tell when a person comes up against a block in their relationship with God, and during conversation it seems as if this kind of thing may be the likely cause.

Occult involvement opens a door to evil in a person's life.

Sometimes when that door is opened more comes in than you bargained for and some kind of deliverance ministry is needed. Once again, this will be beyond the gifts and experience of the group leader. However the leader will be the person in the front line who is able to recognize the problem, know where to go for help, possibly be involved in the ministry, and certainly be continuing to care for the person afterwards. In the Anglican church the ministry of deliverance is carried out under the direction of the bishop, normally through local clergy assisted by a number of advisers in the diocese.

Occult involvement is not the only route by which a person may be open to evil spiritual forces, but it is the most common. If other things lead you to suspect a need for deliverance ministry seek help and guidance from someone who knows about these things.

Family pressure

This is an outside block, not an inside one, but it is still very common. It can be very hard for a partner or family member to understand what happens when a person becomes a Christian. Some of the changes may be for the better – more so, hopefully, as time goes on. But some will definitely be for the worse, as far as family relationships go.

"We used to have lots of time together. Now you're always out at these meetings or at church. You come in at all hours of the night. There's always people in the house that I don't know. You've got these ******* religious tapes playing all the time. You've stopped wanting to do the things we used to do. That church has got more ******* money than it knows what to do with and you still give your housekeeping. And will you please stop nagging me to come to ******* church. I'll go when I'm ready and not before. I'm a ******* Christian just as much as you – it's just that I don't show it in the same way, that's all."

When that kind of thing happens in a serious way, how do we help and advise? Support for the Christian partner is important. But so is simple understanding for the one who is not yet a Christian. It can be very threatening when your husband or wife goes off and gets head over heels involved with people you've never met, and who look at you strangely. It can be unsettling to be constantly invited along to this or that meeting in the hope that you'll be converted.

It does no harm to advise the new Christian in that situation to ease up a bit at home. God needs to be the number one priority now – but the church is not the same as God. A lot of new Christians seem to order their priorities like this:

GOD

CHURCH

FAMILY

When they should be ordered like this:

GOD

FAMILY

CHURCH

God calls us first and foremost to be husbands, fathers, wives, mothers, and only after that to be home group leaders, Sunday School teachers, stewards on Sundays, etc. The more natural a new Christian can be about faith in the home, the greater the affect on the family. There will be a time of testing and teasing – just to see if it's another phase. But that will normally pass. It's after that stage – when a person is settled in their own Christian life – that a real witness in the home begins.

The best thing of all in these situations is for someone in the church, perhaps from the evangelism nurture group, to get to know the whole family. Once the people in the group stop being "those weirdos down at church" and become Tom, Bill and Fred the battle is a long way to being won.

The development of ministry

Pastoral care has its positive side as well. The group leaders are not only involved in trouble-shooting but in ministry development, as each new Christian begins to find his or her place in the church. It's often as that happens that growth begins in earnest.

During my last year in Oxford as a student I attended St Andrew's Church, half a mile out of the centre of town. It was a lively church with good teaching. I went every Sunday and was part of a fellowship group. I even led a study once. But, somehow, I didn't feel part of the family. Until one day, the vicar appealed for people to help cut the grass. I spent one Friday afternoon toiling away with a lawn mower. It was at that point that I began to feel part of the church.

Several weeks later I left Oxford and moved to Durham and into the caretaker's house of a city-centre church, St Margaret's. Right from week one I felt part of the place because from the beginning I was sweeping and cleaning the loos, and locking and unlocking the church hall.

If your church is serious about nurturing new Christians you will need lots of ways in which people can make a start in ministry and make a contribution. Clearly, new Christians cannot be given major responsibility for some time. But there need to be opportunities to become involved in simple, practical tasks — perhaps to read the lessons in church or as part of ministry teams. If all the "ministry slots" are filled by the same people year after year, no wonder new Christians quickly lose interest and drop away. If we are willing to give people responsibility they will quickly grow into that responsibility. If we deny it to them, we will have a church full of spiritual children: used to receiving but unable to give.

Notes to chapter 11

1. A good book to begin with here is Mary Pytches, *Set my people free* (London: Hodder and Stoughton, 1987).
2. A useful book on forgiveness for group members and leaders is the Lion Pocketbook by Vera Sinton, *How can I forgive?* (Oxford: Lion, 1990).

12
Going on growing

Preparing the group for the next stage

"I thank my God every time I remember you. In all my prayers for all of you, I always pray with joy because of your partnership in the gospel from the first day until now, being confident of this, that he who began a good work in you will carry it on to completion until the day of Christ Jesus." Philippians 1:3–6

No good thing lasts forever, not even a group for growing new Christians. Sooner or later the course will come to an end. What is essential is that the growing does not stop when the course ends after ten, fifteen or twenty weeks. How will the individuals within the group move on from here in discipleship, learning, prayer and fellowship?

Most growing churches have found that by far the best way for people to go on growing is a network of small groups of Christians in the church, who meet together for prayer, worship, study and fellowship. However, churches do sometimes struggle over the best way of drawing people from evangelism nurture groups into the home groups.

For each group there are basically two alternatives. The church as a whole needs to employ both options at different times.

Continuing as a home group

This has obvious advantages for the group members. Hopefully, friendships have formed and deepened over the months. People have begun to share openly, perhaps only in the last few weeks of the group's life. If the group has been good, most people will not want to stop meeting together anyway.

There are advantages for the church, too, as the evangelism nurture group gives an excellent base for a new group to be added to existing structures. Generally speaking, this is a much more effective way to add a new group than, say, to divide an existing unit. It has been wisely said that one half of a split home group almost always dies.

The following table gives five points which need to be thought through when the life of the group is to continue in this way.

Going into established home groups

Not every group has a natural cohesion. Also, from time to time, existing home groups lose members or vitality and can be greatly helped by taking in two or three new Christians. It is not advisable, therefore, for each and every evangelism nurture group to become a home group on its own. Sometimes the best thing will be for people to join existing groups.

AN EVANGELISM NURTURE GROUP BECOMES A HOME GROUP

1. **The Leaders** Where possible, the leaders of the new home group should have been part of the evangelism nurture group from the beginning, possibly acting as co-leaders there. Co-leaders should, therefore, be chosen with this possibility in mind, although the decision to take the group on as a home group should not be made until about half-way through its life. Where leaders have to be introduced to take the group on, this should be done at the earliest opportunity.

2. **The Planning** I make it a rule of thumb that, if possible, the group should be told what the plans are about five to six weeks before the course comes to an end. Each person needs to be able to decide for themselves whether to join the new group with the new leaders. Time is needed to think this through.

   It should be emphasized that this will be a new start: a different kind of group; different leaders; and a different kind of commitment. It is very unusual for every single member of an evangelism nurture group to continue in a home group. Although small groups in the church are an excellent thing, they are not for everyone. We should avoid giving the impression that if you do not want to belong to a home group there is something defective about your discipleship.

   Some of the members may wish to join other groups in the church, with family or friends. It may be possible to bring into the new group one or two established Christians who are looking for a transfer from a group which is too big — or who just want a change.

3. **Material** for the new group needs to be carefully chosen. It is no good expecting the group suddenly to have increased in biblical knowledge now they have graduated from nurture to growth. Bible study outlines, which cover very basic subjects, are helpful. So are studies which encourage people to go on sharing and talking about themselves. It is unrealistic to expect many members of the group to be able to lead studies initially, as would be usual in a group of mature Christians. Developing the life of the group in this new way needs sensitivity and patience. With time, many good things grow. If the leaders expect too much too soon, everyone will be discouraged.

4. **Managing Change** For many people, the change from one type of group to another will be difficult, and group members will need help, understanding and support. The new leaders should expect some degree of "bereavement" and looking back, especially if the old group has been successful. The style of the meetings in the evangelism nurture group should change gradually towards the end of the course, so that there is more whole group discussion, more worship and prayer. In other words, the group changes gradually into a new style, rather than suddenly. At the first meeting of the new group, new "ground rules" need to be clearly explained. In our own setting, home groups choose their own names. The process of name-choosing itself becomes an excellent way for a group to establish a new identity.

EVANGELISM NURTURE GROUP MEMBERS JOIN EXISTING GROUPS

1. **Clusters** As a new Christian it's very hard to join an existing group on your own. To send people out from an evangelism nurture group singly, to different groups, is not a good idea; the majority simply will not become established in their new groups. It's much better to divide the group into clusters of three to five people, possibly with a co-leader in each. The new Christians then make some impact on the receiving group and have mutual support as they are settling in.

2. **Planning** Again, the planning needs to begin five or six weeks before the evangelism nurture group ends. If possible, every person needs to be introduced individually to their new home group leader. The new group needs time to pray and to prepare to receive new people. It would be somewhat daunting for a new Christian to be pitched into the middle of a twenty week series on the minor prophets.

   Generally speaking, people will be much more hesitant about joining an existing group than continuing with the same group they have come to know. The old fears will re-surface: about feeling ignorant; being shy in front of others; being expected to pray aloud, etc. It can help to have one or two home group leaders or members visit the evangelism nurture group at this point, to explain what the groups are all about and to encourage people to join.

3. **The first meetings** after the new members have joined need to be planned with special care. In terms of its development, with three or four new members the group is now a new group. People will not share or discuss openly with folk they do not know. Established members may suddenly become quiet. New members will take their cue from this. The group needs to go back to simple sharing and history-giving for at least part of the meeting. There needs to be time given to induction and readjustment in the group. If all this is rightly handled over the initial weeks, the group will soon grow back again into a close fellowship. If the simple principles of group dynamics are ignored, the group simply will not gel together.

4. **Pastoral Care** The tasks of the evangelism nurture group
    leaders do not end on the last evening of the course. It is this
    team's job to ensure that everyone who wants to join is
    settled in to a home group; that the group suits them well
    and there are no serious personality clashes; and that they
    are prepared to go on growing into the future.

Home groups and training in the Church

Through the whole of this book our attention has been focused
on the central part of the cracker structures for growth, identified
in chapters two and three.

As any one church grows – and as churches all over the country
begin to grow again – our attention will be focused more and
more to the right-hand side of the structure. How do we take
people on from here? We have learned lessons about how people
become Christians and established in faith. But how do things
develop from here? The biggest single area for growth in the
church, in the second half of the 1990s and beyond, will not be
evangelism – which we are now learning to do effectively – but
adult, Christian education and training.

Home groups

Establishing effective home groups is key here. The vision of
home groups – and expectations of group members – vary
enormously from church to church, and usually within churches.
Yet a common understanding is important.

As with evangelism nurture groups, a small group structure
for Christians develops with history, culture and size of the
church. There is no single model which fits every situation. Some
new home group leaders, in our own context, recently agreed
the following vision for the groups.

A home group is a place . . . . .

. . . where the worship is powerful

. . . where the prayer is effective

. . . where we learn from God's word

. . . where gifts are developed

. . . where we care for each other

. . . where everyone feels at home

. . . where everyone is growing

. . . where people have fun

. . . where you can be encouraged

. . . where we can be family

. . . where we can reach out together

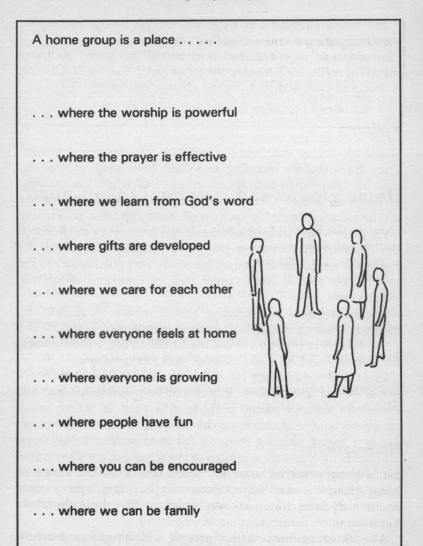

The vision statement is long, but we are trying to describe something complex: the church in microcosm.

Involvement in evangelism nurture will inevitably lead any church to review and develop the small group structures. Growth in any part of the church means change elsewhere.

Training

Home groups are excellent for worship, fellowship and prayer. They are useful for learning, especially Bible study. However, they also have their limitations, most of all when the majority of the group are new Christians. If the group depends for learning on the members teaching each other, not a great deal of learning takes place where individuals do not yet know very much about the Christian life. Even in a group of established Christians, the freshness can go out of group Bible study very quickly unless the leaders are able to put a great deal of time and effort into preparation.

Other mediums for training and Christian education are needed. After an evangelism nurture course people still need a great deal more input on living the Christian life, to equip them for ministry and to guide in work and relationships.

Ideas and suggestions for different subjects and formats are given on the table below. It may not be possible for any one church to attempt many of these in a year. In many urban situations outside resources can be drawn in. Larger churches can act as a useful training resource for their smaller neighbours. Deaneries or ecumenical groups of churches can combine forces for a programme of courses. There are a whole range of possibilities. It is vital that this element in the church's programme is there in some way, however small, so that the growth can continue.

The format for each type of course will depend on a whole number of things: the church timetable; buildings being available; someone to lead the group; whether you are working with other churches. The following table gives four different suggestions for format, which are tried and tested:

TRAINING IDEAS – SUBJECTS

1. Learning about the faith
Learning to pray
Understanding the New Testament
Understanding the Old Testament
The gifts of the Holy Spirit
Outlines in Church history
In-depth studies of biblical books
Reasons to believe – the evidence for faith

2. Equipped for ministry
Personal faith-sharing
Door-to-door visiting
Leading groups
Leadership training
Working with children and young people
Counselling
Pastoral care
The ministry of healing
Serving God on the PCC
Leading prayers in church

3. Life-based courses
Marriage preparation and enrichment
Bringing up a family
Coming to terms with bereavement
Recovering from a divorce
Being a Christian at work
Retirement and the Christian
Handling teenagers
Managing stress

TRAINING IDEAS – FORMAT

1. **Six Evenings** We ran a series of courses at St George's on Sunday evenings after church from 8.30 until 10.00 p.m., with a cup of coffee available between the end of evening worship and the start of the session. The most popular were a twelve-week course on the ministry of healing and a six-week programme called "Learning to Pray". The teaching was structured. There was a practical dimension. Notes accompanied the talks and sessions were taped for those who missed an evening.

2. **Training Conferences** These have developed over the last two years. The idea is to take a larger chunk of time and study one issue in depth. Normally the conferences run from Friday evening to Saturday morning, and are sometimes followed by a celebration on the Saturday night. They include time for worship and ministry, as well as input. The input is backed-up by printed notes and, again, the sessions are taped. So far, each one has been an excellent time for in-depth learning. The week-ends are easier to fit into a busy church programme and provide a better opportunity for people in other churches to come and join in.

3. **A Lent Training School** When I was a curate in North London, the seven church Local Ecumenical Project there mounted a series of very successful training schools each Lent. Each year, six courses were offered on different nights of the week and in different venues around town. Each course was either led by two ministers from different churches or chaired by one person, with different speakers for each subject. Subjects ranged from very practical to the very theoretical. Each course had its own style and feel. Each year over 200 people attended, showing what a desire there is to learn more about the faith.

4. **A Church Training Centre** If the major task of the 1990s is adult education and training, we need to think big and to be prepared. Our own church is completing the refurbishment of the former vicarage as a centre for Christian education and training. Our vision is to mount a continuous series of courses throughout the year, to provide a secure foundation for Christian faith, belief and ministry over many years to come.

Review

During my first pastoral studies lecture at theological college, the tutor impressed us with the thought that we do not learn by experience. We learn by reflecting on that experience. There are lessons we can learn from everything which happens in the life of a church, especially the failures.

As you come to the end of leading a group for nurture and evangelism, make sure there is a process of review, so the lessons can be taken forward. Establish good lines of feedback from the group. In the right context, a questionnaire can be helpful. We all value and need encouragement, but don't be afraid of negative feedback either.

Learn from all that has happened, positive and negative, and then build in the changes for the next group and beyond. The way people become Christians and are nurtured within the church is one of the most important dimensions of church life. Time invested in this area is always time well spent.

A last word to leaders

Those called to be involved in sharing the faith with enquirers and in the nurture of new Christians have one of the highest callings in the whole of Christian ministry. Often we will feel inadequate to the task; that even our best is not enough. And, of course, we will be absolutely correct. It is God who gives the growth. All our finest gifts, skills, abilities and planning mean nothing unless God himself is at work, gently drawing men and women to new life in Christ. Yet when God himself is at work anything can happen.

''Now to him who is able to do immeasurably more than all we ask or imagine, according to his power that is at work within us, to him be glory in the church and in Christ Jesus throughout all generations, for ever and ever! Amen.''

PART FOUR

Resources

13
Addresses, books, etc.

Published material for course members

My experience is that there's not a lot of it about. Six months ago, while I was writing the first part of *Growing New Christians*, I walked into a large Christian bookshop in Cambridge.

"Hello," I said, "I'm just looking for material on adult Christian nurture, confirmation preparation, that kind of thing."

"If I were you," said the man, "I'd go away and write something."

"Funny you should say that . . ." I replied.

Seven possible courses are listed here for new Christians, including *Christians for Life*. Two of the courses listed were only published in 1991. Whilst *Christian Basics* and *Follow me* have done something to fill the immense need for this material, I believe far more thinking, writing and investment by the Church and publishers is needed. Here are the seven (in no particular order). Details of the session outlines are given in chapter six.

1. Christian Basics (CPAS: 1991)

Christian Basics is a well-produced and packaged training kit for nurture groups and for group leaders. The pack includes six videos on the six central themes of the course, together with written material for the twenty-four themes listed. This written material includes handouts for group members and a leader's guide. The kit also contains notes for thirty Bible studies; advice for church leaders on course design, and ideas for training group leaders. Many churches have bought the kit already. If you haven't and want a flexible, in-depth resource for adult Christian nurture, then *Basics* is one to consider.

haven't and want a flexible, in-depth resource for adult Christian nurture, then *Basics* is one to consider.

2. Saints Alive, John Finney and Felicity Lawson (Anglican Renewal Ministries: 1990)

Saints Alive was originally developed as a helpful course for drawing those who were already Christians into a deeper experience of the Life of the Spirit. However, it has been used to good effect in many parishes as Christian nurture material. The full kit contains a leader's handbook; workbooks for course members, and video support for some of the sessions.

3. Follow Me, edited by Stephen Cottrell and Martin Warner (Additional Curate's Society: 1991)

Follow Me is a very well produced package from the Anglo-Catholic tradition based on the catechumenate approach. As well as a leader's guide the kit contains teaching material for adults, teenagers and young children in the form of workbooks; liturgical material for different stages of the journey, and ideas for prayer and practical projects. The basic workbook format means that the course will not be suitable for those churches or communities which do not want to lay great emphasis (or any emphasis) on traditional Anglo-Catholic doctrines and practices. However, anyone involved in designing or leading a course for Christian nurture would benefit from referring to *Follow Me*.

4. Christians for Life

This is the evangelism nurture course developed in St George's and referred to (often) in this book. The basic pack consists of a two-page leader's guide and a two-sided handout for each of the fifteen course sessions. The handouts contain group exercises; outlines of the teaching, and ideas for prayer and worship. The session sheets are not numbered and can be used in any combination; or your own sheet substituted for a particular session. *Christians for Life* is already in use in a number of other churches and is proving a helpful tool for evangelism and nurture there.

Copies are available by post from St George's House, Lee Mount, Halifax, HX3 5BT at a cost of £5 for the basic pack, and an additional £15 for a licence to copy the handouts.

The final three of the seven are not sold as courses but as books, and are based on preparation for confirmation. I hope what you have read so far has put you off basing your course on a traditional "Confirmation Book". If you're still not convinced, or if you want to base your own course or talks on something published, I would recommend the following:

5. To Be Confirmed by Gavin Reid (London: Hodder and Stoughton, 1977)

If your group can cope with a book at all (and many can't), and if your nurture model is still that of confirmation, *To be confirmed* is one of the simplest and easiest to read, and contains questions for discussion at the end of each chapter.

6. Confirmation Notebook by Hugh Montefiore (London: SPCK, 1984)

This is not so much a book to read as an extremely useful series of headings for short talks.

7. Your Confirmation by John Stott (London: Hodder and Stoughton, 1991)

A very attractively designed book with colour pictures, and one which can be placed with confidence into the hands of any enquirer or new Christian who reads books. The study guide (written by Lance Pierson) could be used as a basis for group discussions.

Published material for course leaders

Not much has been written on the general subject of **growing new Christians**. I have been helped by the chapter in Michael Green's book *Evangelism in the Local Church* (London: Hodder and Stoughton, 1990) and also by Peter Ball *Adult Believing* (Oxford: Mowbray, 1988).

Several excellent books are available on **groups and group dynamics**. *Growing Christians in Small Groups* by John Mallison (London: Scripture Union, 1990) is particularly good.

The CPAS Christian Basics course gives a very helpful list of useful reference books for leaders on the different subjects covered, and especially recommends, as I do myself, the *Lion Handbook of Christian Belief* (Oxford: Lion Publishing, 1982).

One of Michael Green's helpful suggestions is to develop a basics library for new Christians, which can be kept in a box and brought to the group each week. Whether it will work or not depends on how good your group are at returning things. The only time I tried it all of the books disappeared the first week and only two came back.

I have found the following helpful for enquirers or new Christians:

Testimony books: *Freed for Life* by Rita Nightingale (London: Marshall Pickering, 1982); *The Cross behind bars*, by Jenny Cooke, (Eastbourne: Kingsway, 1983).

Lion Pocketbooks are available for about £1.25 each and cover a wide range of subjects, both evangelistic and pastoral.

Books for Enquirers are also useful. A general all-rounder here is *It makes sense* by Steve Gaukroger (London: Scripture Union, 1987).

Video and Audio Tapes can also be good for a lending library. *Jesus of Nazareth*, starring Robert Powell, is an excellent resource for building into group meetings or for lending out. David Watson's series *Jesus then and now* can also be useful in the right setting. Lending worship tapes can be a means of building people up in faith; as can tapes of the course sessions themselves or of particular sermons in church.

Group building exercises

As every good preacher needs a good battery of illustrations, so every good group leader needs a store of exercises to be used in different ways in different settings. To give you a start, or to add to your stock, here are some of the ones I have used in *Christians for Life* over the years. You will find others in the courses listed above; in books about group work (both Christian and secular); and in many Bible study booklets written for adults and teenagers.

1. Getting to Know You (1) (Session Numbers refer to *Christians for Life* – see pp. 218f for an outline of the course.)

Divide into pairs and interview your partner. Find out who they are, where they live, what their work and family circumstances are. Find out, if you can, why they have come to this group. Each person then takes it in turn to introduce their partner to the whole course.

Here are some questions to guide you:

- Your name
- Your home situation
- Your work situation
- What's the best thing that has happened to you in the last year?
- Why have you joined this group?

Note: Most people find it much easier to talk about their partner to a group of strangers than they would to talk about themselves.

2. Leaving home (2)

In small groups share your own memories of living at home and of childhood. What were the best things about childhood for you?. Was there anything unusual about your own childhood? At what age did you leave home? How did it feel?

Note: This exercise is a preliminary to a study of the prodigal son.

3. How much do you know about Jesus? (3)

Share together in small groups what you already know about Jesus:

- What attracts you about Jesus of Nazareth?
- What questions do you have about him?
- How much, if any, of the gospels have you read?
- Has your impression of Jesus changed very much as you have grown older?

Note: This one can be adapted as an introduction to other subjects such as the Holy Spirit, the Bible, prayer, etc.

4. Becoming a Christian (6)

Share together the story of your journey to faith. Are you a Christian? How did you come to faith?

Can you say what is wrong with these descriptions of what a Christian is?

- I went to Sunday School
- I'm as good as he is
- I believe in God
- We were married in church
- I enjoy *Songs of Praise*
- I was baptized as a baby
- I'm not anything else
- My wife goes

How would you describe a Christian?

5. The Ten Commandments (11)

In groups of three or four (and without looking) write down as many of the ten commandments as you can.

Of the ones you have named, which three are the most often broken today?

Look up the full list in Exodus 20 and check your answers.

6. Your picture of the church (9)

Draw on a piece of scrap paper a picture of the church as you see it (tortoise, army etc.).

Now put yourself in the picture and talk about what you have drawn with the group.

Note: We dropped this particular exercise after several groups found drawing a picture the most threatening thing they had to do in the whole course.

7. Into action together (12)

Imagine there is no church at all in the neighbouring community of Someplace. The members of your group are sent out by your church to plant a new congregation in that area.

You have fifteen minutes to work out how you would begin; what your priorities as a church are, and especially what gifts you have in your group for ministry in the new situation.

- What are the essential tasks which need to be done?
- Who will exercise which ministry?

Everyone in the group must play a part. You have no premises and a grant of just £500.

Note: The group leader(s) should leave the room during this exercise and listen to a report back after fifteen minutes.

8. A Christian at work (13)

Share with each other in small groups the story of your working life.

- How old were you when you started work?
- What different jobs have you had?
- Which have you enjoyed the most?
- Are you happy in what you are doing now?
- How has being a Christian made a difference at work?
- How has being a Christian changed your attitude to money?